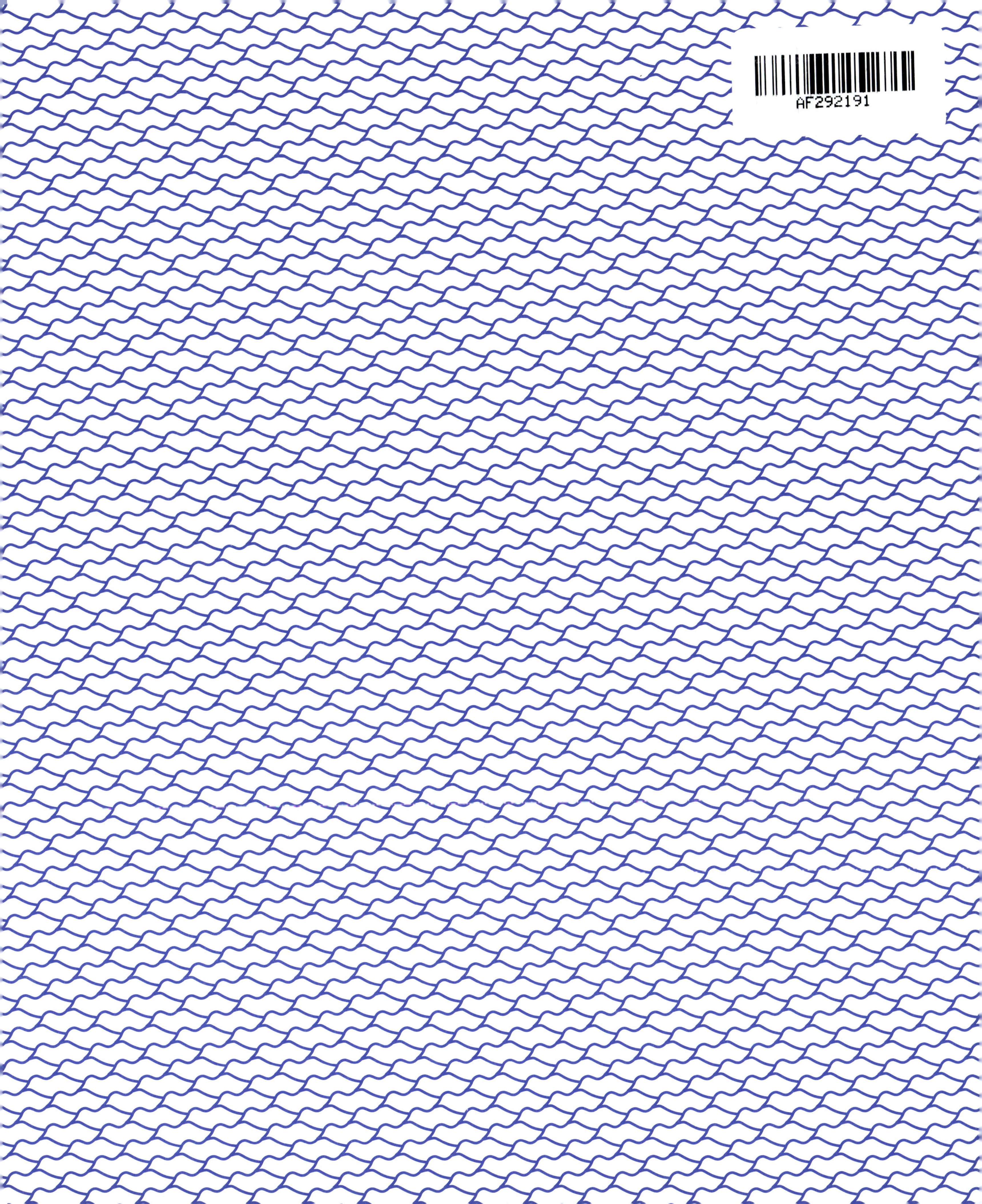
AF292191

perched

FELEKŞAN ONAR

PERCHED
ISBN 978–1–911300–98–4

PHOTOS
David von Becker
Serkan Eldeleklioğlu
Johannes Kramer
Dario J. Laganà
Daniel Oduntan
Dr. Anke Scharrahs
Mo Zaboli

DESIGN
Studio PUL
hello@studiopul.com

BOOK COORDINATOR
Yavuz Parlar

TRANSLATION & PROOFREADING
Dr. Sujatha Chandrasekaran

EDITION
1500 Copies

PUBLISHER / DISTRIBUTOR
Paul Holberton Publishing
89 Borough High Street, London SE1 1NL
T +44 (0) 20 7407 0809
sales@paulholberton.com | www.paulholberton.com

CONTENTS

To my husband and forever supporter,
and my beloved daughters whose love
I cherish and drives me forward.

FOREWORD

Felekşan Onar

In April of 2017, as millions of Syrian refugees took shelter in my home country, I arrived in Berlin to work at Berlin Glassworks with the intention to blow some closed winged birds into plaster moulds. The sculptural feel of the abstract model I had already started to work on back in Istanbul had already taken me into a journey back in time to when I read *Birds Without Wings* by Louis de Bernières with tears in my eyes. I grew up on the Aegean coast of Anatolia, and Louis's story about the period following the First World War, when families and neighbours found themselves thrown across the newly established borders of Turkey and Greece, was one very close to my heart. Today, I am witnessing a similar tragedy as war-fleeing Syrian families find themselves on the streets of Istanbul, not knowing where to go or what to do next. Simply perched on side walks, like birds without wings.

Glass continues to surprise me each time. When we started blowing the glass into plaster moulds, the first pieces to take form were so fragile and tender, because the surfaces picked up the uneven details of the plaster. I moved from blowing ambers, amethysts and greys to blues, greens, pinks, while sprinkling various shades of iridescent coloured glass powder and particles on those closed wings. The first display of the resulting pieces was so captivating that Nadania Idriss, founder of Berlin Glassworks, encouraged and facilitated a conversation between myself and Prof. Dr. Stefan Weber, the director of Museum für Islamische Kunst at the Pergamon Museum, together with curator Miriam Kühn. As a result, the initial installation of *Perched* was presented in the Aleppo Room of the museum in 2018. Such an intervention had not been exercised often in the museum before. The simple placement of the birds on the floor of the Aleppo Room complemented the background and placed the story in its correct context – this not only appealed to many visitors, but was also the reason for conservator Dr. Anke Scharrachs to encourage me to connect with other museums exhibiting Damascene interiors.

Contrary to their creation, the glass birds' story took a paradoxical angle as they travelled to London, to the Victoria and Albert Museum, where Mariam Rosser-Owen, curator at the Islamic Middle East Galleries, installed them in the Jameel Gallery in time for Refugee Week. While the museum was providing temporary shelter to these fragile birds, the idea of contacting Louis de Bernières came up for the first time during a conversation with my friend İdil Kartal. Up until then, Louis, for me, embodied just the book *Birds Without Wings* and not the person behind it, therefore it had not occurred to me to reach out to him. Now that the birds were in London and Louis lived closed by, meeting him became a reality. When I reached out to him and asked him to join me in a public conversation to take place at the museum, he replied back right away, so here we were, the writer of the book that has inspired my work, face to face observing the glass installation and talking about our journeys.

It was around this time that it dawned on me that *Perched* was no longer simply a stunning installation in a museum, but had become a fundamental work in my career as a glass artist. Conversations with my good friend Füsun Eczacıbaşı, encouragement from Banu and Hakan Çarmıklı, and the continuous mentorship of Mecka Baumeister, conservator at the Metropolitan Museum in New York, together with media strategist Defne Aydıntaşbaş, also in New York City, led me to start thinking about turning this story into a book. However, it is one thing to start thinking about making a book and another challenge actually realising it. If it were not the delicate navigation Merve Çağlar kindly offered me over our weekly lunches, midnight phone conversations and back and forth emails, none of this would have been possible in such insightful form. Merve respected and honoured my work and believed in my cry for this story to be heard.

As *Perched* was on view at the Victoria and Albert Museum, I reached out to the museum's head of content, Tom Windross, who connected me with my current publisher, Paul Holberton, and I started formulating the necessary steps for the book with him. Soon after, Yavuz Parlar joined my book team as the project coordinator. Nadania again introduced me to another specialist, photography artist Dario J. Laganà, who captured the souls of my birds in his shots. And soon after, the talented graphic designer Amir Jamshidi, who had relocated to Istanbul, also joined the team.

As the exhibition at the Victoria and Albert Museum came to an end, I was still having discussions with Dresden and travelling there for the first time to meet Stefanie Bach, the curator at the Staatlichen Kunstsammlungen. I had seen pictures of the panels from the Damascus Room, but seeing it in reality was something else. This wooden reception room with the beautiful, hand-painted patterns and figures on its panels was made around the turn of the nineteenth century in Damascus and later purchased by a German collector, who brought it to Germany in early 1900s. However, the room had never been fully reassembled since it departure from Damascus. Years of conservation work on the Room were finally coming to an end, and Stefanie was as excited as I am to see *Perched* installed in the room for its first fully reconstructed public viewing. With the blessing and support of Léontine Meijer-van Mensch, Director of the Museum, we decided that the next touch-down for the birds would be there in September 2020.

Setting a date for such a special occasion motivated both myself as well as all the contributors even more towards completion of the book. This book could not exist without the written contributions of Stefanie Bach, Nadania Idriss, Mariam Rosser-Owen and Prof. Dr. Stefan Weber, who had already been involved in the creation and exhibition of *Perched* as works of glass art, and were now kindly offering their personal time to become involved in the book project of *Perched*. *The Debt to the Birds*, a short story written by Louis de Bernières specially for this book, eternally crowned the content. I am forever grateful. Since the works have been shown mainly in English- and German-speaking locations, Yavuz and I decided to present the book content in both English and German versions, and that is when Dr. Sujatha Chandrasekaran joined the book team to provide her valuable professional assistance in translations. Through Melanie Courbet, my gallerist in New York City, I connected with Glenn Adamson, who finally rounded off the book with an interview.

So what now? What is next for me? What is next for *Perched*? First of all, I am content .... As I was making these beautiful birds, I wanted the viewers to look at them with a smile on their faces even though the birds' stories are grim. I yearned for the world to witness the reality of the Syrian refugee crisis through these fragile glass birds. Therefore, I had an urge for them to travel to locations, and they have. Each location where they were shown acquired a flock of seven birds for their permanent collections, which means the birds will be with the public for years to come. So I am also grateful. I am grateful for having found an art that enables me to speak my heart.

At any point in time, there are 45 million displaced people around the world. Unfortunately, these numbers only increase as economical and political power plays escalate around the globe. One could feel helpless facing such tragedies as an individual, but as an artist I have a peaceful heart knowing I can create consciousness in communities through my practice. I shall continue to do so...

ON BEING PERCHED

Nadania Idriss
Founder and CEO of Berlin Glassworks

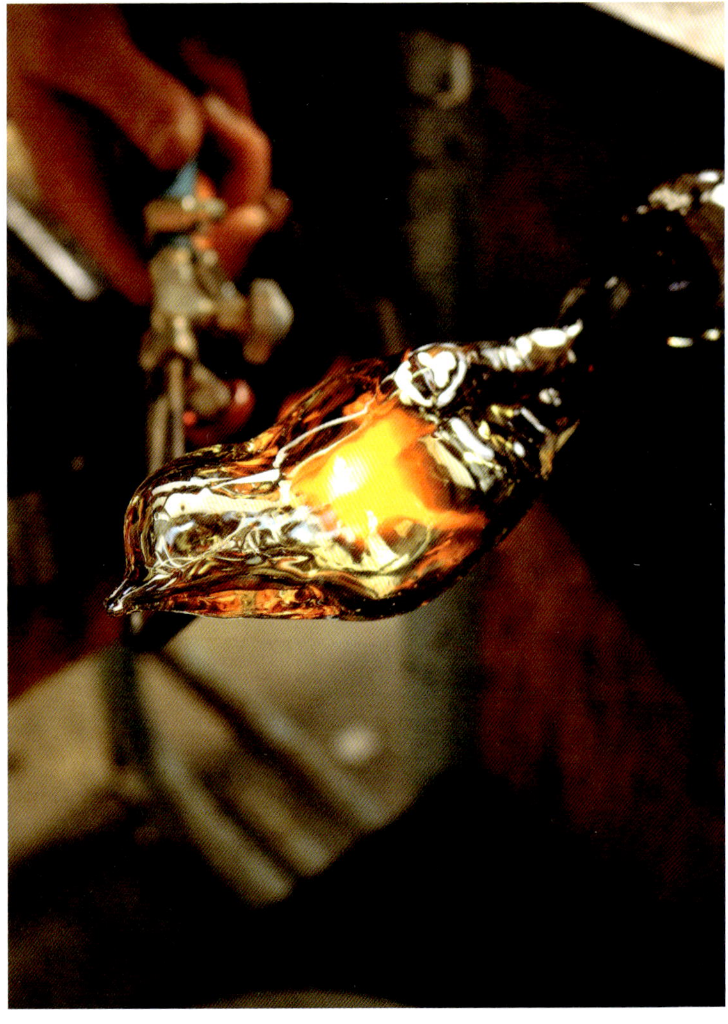

The Berlin Glassworks is a maker's space, where we assist artists in realizing their concepts in tangible forms of glass. In doing so, I am fortunate to be invited into their brilliant minds – even though their visit is often short, too short, and, as a budding business, we must move forward onto the next project. Sometimes the artists and our projects overlap. However, this was not the case when Felekşan Onar chose to work with us and explained her ideas behind *Perched* one afternoon in April 2017.

My father comes from Damascus, Syria, a country I was able to travel to a handful of times in the 1990s and early 2000s. It was beautiful. We imagined a world in which governments would be democratically chosen, and therefore I was excited about the prospect of change in my father's country of origin. I never imagined that when a new generation would step up to elicit change, it would result in a civil war that would tear this beautiful country into ruins. I am flabbergasted each time I read the stories and statistics of the people who have had to flee the country, and have perished in their plight to provide safety for their children.

In September 2015, when Germany opened its borders to the thousands of refugees, the Berlin Glassworks team created a new outreach programme for children that would help alleviate – at least for a short period – the memory of escape that they must now carry with them. It was also the beginning of an internal shift, as I began to experience watching people of my own heritage be reduced to conversations revolving around racism, stereotyping and sentimentality. How can we help and what does our help actually represent? How is art supposed to foster a culture of peace when there is so much pain involved?

Joy, we learned, is the outcome of this process. The workshops take around two hours and during those one hundred and twenty minutes the participants have been freed of the burden of losing their homes, the journey it took for them to reach a safer place, and the new burdens that have been thrown upon them in their new location. These words are not from observation, but from speaking frankly with the children and their parents.

Through art important matters are communicated – whether we should address the emergency situation of our climate, or whether we want to remind ourselves to be joyful. In our quest to build a culture of peace through art, however, there were still unanswered questions. There was something running deeper in these families than we were able to reach with what we had to offer. The experience of witnessing a tragedy of this scale for the very culture from which I descend was not that simple to understand and articulate, not until Felekşan came to us to create *Perched*.

I used to tell my friends that if one wants to visit the Middle East, one should start one's journey in Syria. Our senses are activated through the colours of the landscape and the myriad of spices, soaps, crafts that unfold as one strolls through the markets of Aleppo and Damascus. Thousands of years of civilizations have inhabited this land, all of which is ever-so-present in its juxtaposition with contemporary society.

Felekşan was emotional as she stood in front of me talking of the innumerable number of refugees that have fled to Turkey. Was the rest of the world aware of this? Do they know the implications of displacement? She does, through her childhood growing up in a village near Greece, which put her in contact with people who had been part of the great population exchange in the 1920s. When Louis de Bernières published *Birds Without Wings* (2004), Felekşan understood the context at a very deep level. It was from this perspective that she wanted to tell the story of displacement through the allegory of swallows who have lost their wings.

I was motionless myself, as her words resonated so strongly. She was touching a part of me that I did not know how to articulate, and, at the same time, answering some of the questions that haunted me. I wanted to help her convey this story, which inhabits similar layers for the majority of us who live outside of this tragedy. I feel guilt for having the privilege of a visa to reside in Germany and the privilege of imposing expectations on myself to succeed. Roadblocks are a matter of personal circumstance, they are not forced on me via political, societal circumstances or due to war. I am of the same culture and yet I am something else. The installation *Perched* matters. It matters, because it will resonate with others as it did with me.

The installation, composed of 99 handcrafted, delicate glass swallows is simultaneously joyful and reflective. The pigments and surface texture of each unique sculpture recall the multitude of hues that unfold in Syrian daily life; and yet these swallows sit patiently, heads tilted downward as they try to understand the situation that has befallen them.

ON THE MEANING OF LIFE IN EXILE FOR PEOPLE AND CULTURAL PROPERTY

Stefanie Bach
Curator, Staatlichen Kunstsammlungen Dresden

In November 2019, the Damascus Room in the Dresden Museum für Völkerkunde was reopened to the public on a permanent basis as a restoration workshop. From autumn 2020, the room display will be enhanced by the contemporary artistic intervention *Perched*, created by Turkish artist Felekşan Onar. The framework of the historical reception room contrasts with the modernity of the artistic work, allowing the museum to enter into a dialogue with visitors on questions of exile, identity, homeland and flight.

The wooden room panelling fashioned around 1810–11 in Damascus, then part of the Ottoman Empire. Towards the end of the nineteenth century, it was purchased by art collector Karl Ernst Osthaus and removed to Germany. Following his death, the disassembled panels were discovered by one of his heirs in 1930 and bequeathed to the Dresden Museum für Völkerkunde. For decades, they remained in museum storage. Conservation and restoration of the panels, which had been packed in newspaper, commenced only in 1997. The elaborate wooden interior with its paintings, relief ornamentation and appliqués of metal leaf is still undergoing this process. Indeed, the room has never been fully reassembled and presented since its original dismantling in Damascus. Now, for the first time since its completion, it will be possible to enter the Damascus Room in its original composition and coloration here in Dresden.

The wall and ceiling panels once adorned a reception room of a Damascene house in the historic city.

One entered the room from a planted inner courtyard with a water basin. The assemblage of 113 individual pieces presents a detailed composition of city landscapes, bouquets of flowers, bowls of fruit and Arabic inscriptions, all attesting to the original owner's considerable financial investment. In addition to the wall and ceiling décor, such rooms were also furnished with expensive carpets, porcelain, books and other accessories, all aimed at heightening the atmosphere of prestige when receiving guests.

In the second half of the nineteenth century major changes in the design of houses and thus also of such reception rooms took place in Damascus. More and more European elements found their way into the interior design and decoration. As a result, many of the wooden wall and ceiling panels that had been used were removed, sanded down or completely repainted. The Damascus Room in the Dresden Museum für Völkerkunde has escaped this process and thus represents one of the few interiors of which the original colour scheme has been preserved to this day. And so the reconstruction of the historic reception room will provide an insight into the civic culture of one of the oldest trading cities in the world.

The presentation of the Damascus Room in Dresden gains additional meaning in light of the ongoing conflict in Syria. Furthermore, the installation of the intervention *Perched* by Turkish glass artist and designer Felekşan Onar inside this room allows the museum to offer an artistic approach to the questions of homeland, exile and flight.

Felekşan Onar is currently living in Istanbul. Over 500,000 Syrians are stranded in the Turkish metropolis as a result of the Syrian Civil War. The consequences of the war are particularly visible in the Pera district, where Onar has her atelier. Onar's personal experience in Turkey as well as her own encounter with Louis de Bernières's novel *Birds Without Wings* provided the inspiration for *Perched*. The artistic installation consists of 99 glass birds, all wingless, meaning that they can neither fly nor leave their current place. The birds represent the thousands of Syrian refugees in Turkey who cannot reach their new home or leave their exile, who do not know what the future holds. They are thus in a stalemate, with no way out.

Onar's installation stands all the more for the millions of Syrian refugees who have found a new home – both in Turkey as well as in Europe. Each of the birds has its own distinguishing features. While each hand-fashioned bird stems from the same master model – a clay bird sculpted by the artist herself – each has been varied during the production process to acquire a unique character. The design, color, structure and transparent surfaces lend the birds distinctive nuances, like the millions of people who fled the Syrian Civil War to seek safety, each with their individual lives, biographies and stories. Each must remain in their current exile, not knowing what is to come.

The reconstructed Damascus Room in Dresden echoes this sentiment. Like the refugees, the room also comes from a region that has experienced massive loss and destruction of its cultural property. The Dresden Museum für Völkerkunde has, in a sense, become a place of exile for this room. But can and will it remain a part of the museum collection forever? It is kept and restored here, it can serve people as a source of comfort, preserve

View of the Damascus Room.
Photo: Mo Zaboli
© Staatliche Kunstsammlungen Dresden

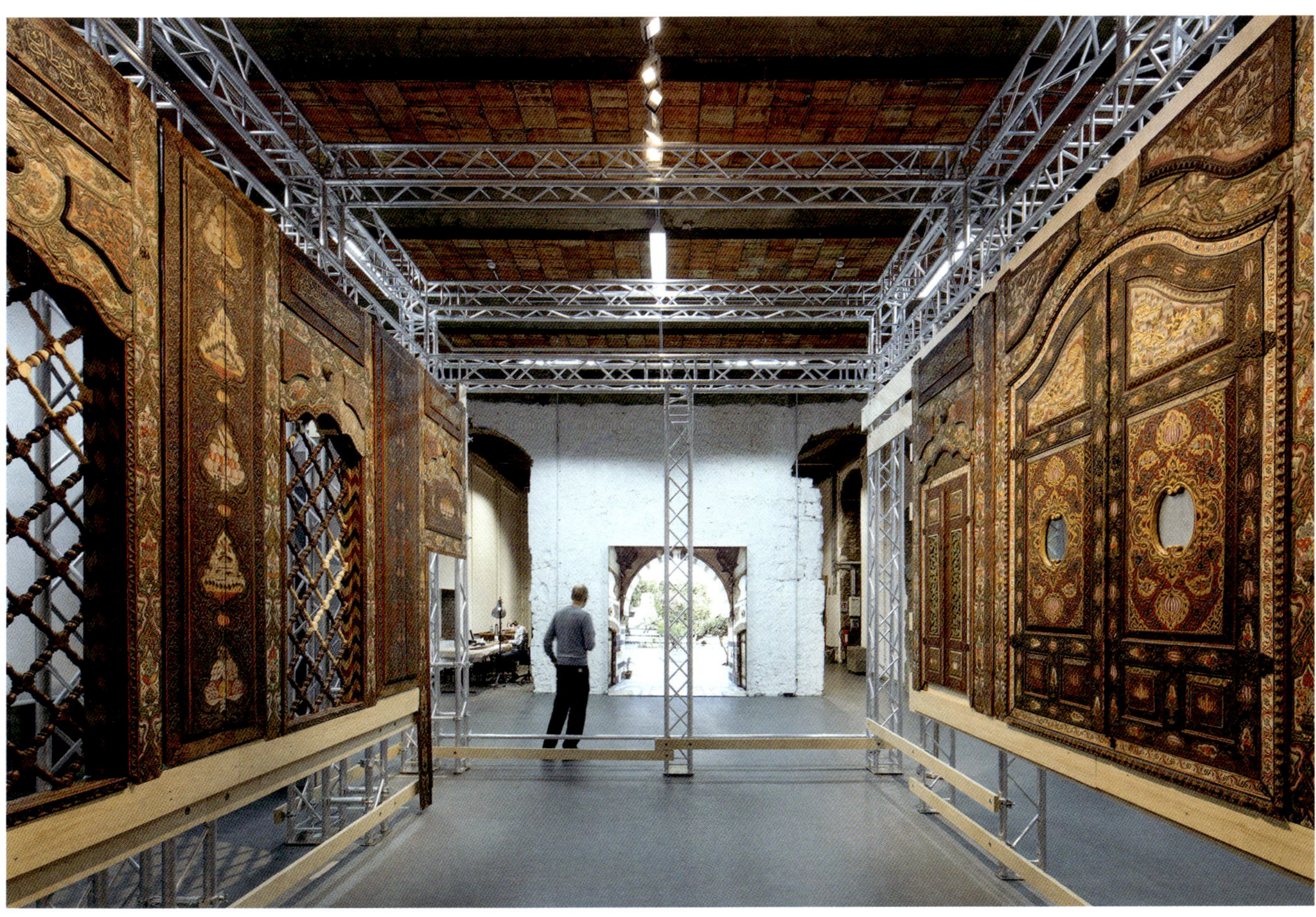

their cultures and identities, recall memories of their homeland or even function as a meeting place for the Syrian community. It can grow beyond being simply a space of knowledge to playing an important role in a community.

Here in Germany, here in Dresden, the Damascus Room can help promote new perspectives by which to counter prevalent clichés about refugees and thus take a stand against xenophobia and racism. The three ethnological museums in Saxony, which include the Dresden Museum für Völkerkunde, preserve evidence of histories, cultural diversity, art and religions for future generations. The museums function as part of the world and its political situation today and must therefore react accordingly. Therefore modern recurrences of xenophobia - i.e. fear and rejection of the supposed 'other' - underscore the importance of the Saxony museums' educational mandate.

Felekşan Onar's *Perched* allows the museum to present these perspectives in order to facilitate a critical approach to questions of exile and homeland, multiple identities, flight, memory and life in limbo. Otherwise, we may question what is implied when Europe closes its borders to thousands of refugees and leaves them in a place without rights or possessions, limiting their capacity to act.

Detail from the Damascus Room.
Photo: Dr. Anke Scharrahs
© Staatliche Kunstsammlungen Dresden

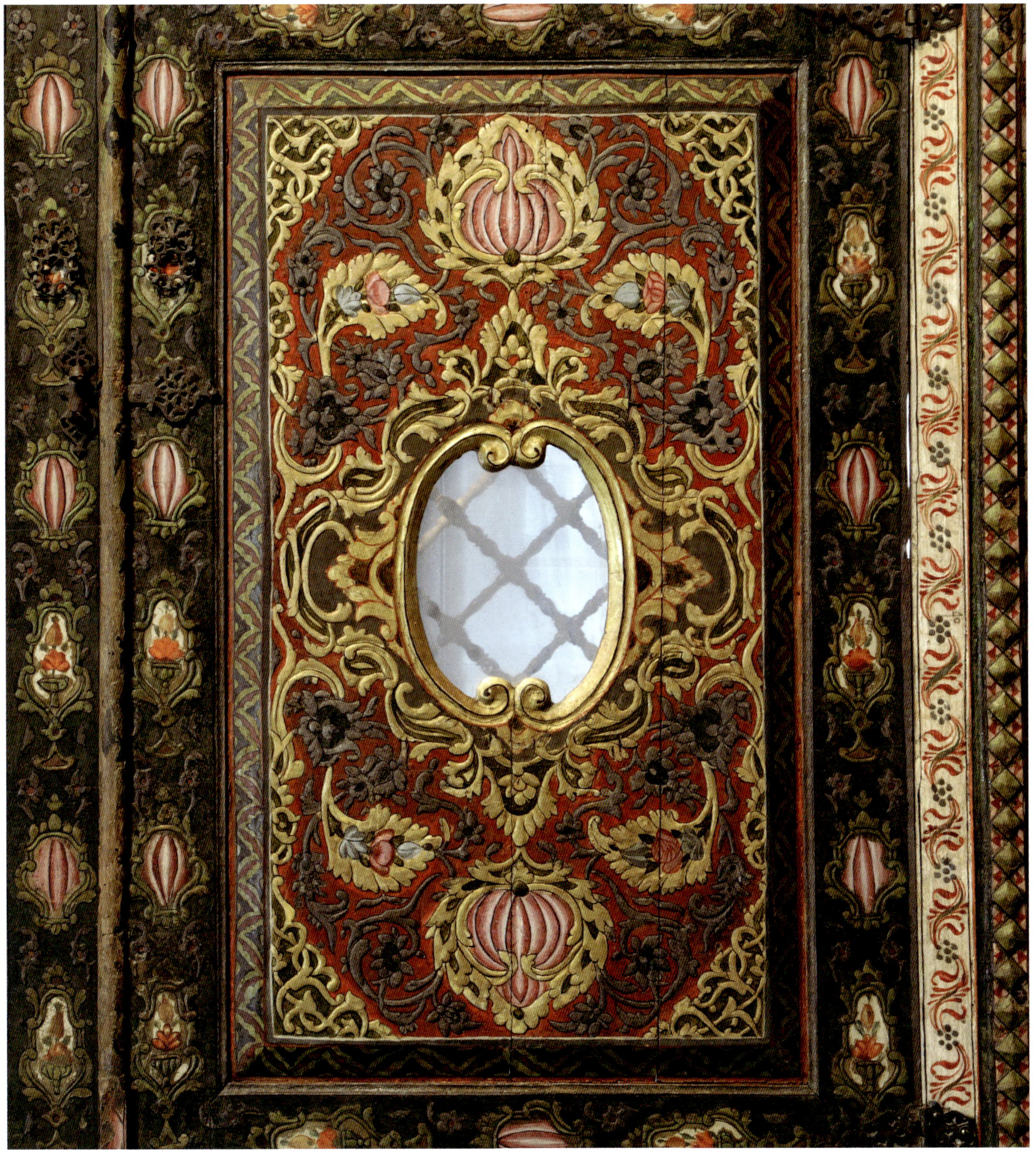

THE DEBT
TO THE BIRDS

There was once a boy of twelve years who was given a gun by his father, who had once been a soldier and naturally wanted his little boy to become like him.

The weapon was the same one that his own father had given him. He took the boy into the garden and showed him how to shoot standing up, kneeling, and lying down. He told him that you must take aim and shoot quickly, because otherwise your arms begin to ache and your aim wavers. He said that for a soldier it was safest and most accurate if you lie down as you shoot, and you spread your legs like this, and you put your cheek on the stock of the gun like this, and always remember that you don't pull the trigger, you squeeze your whole hand firmly, and that way there is much less of a leap when the round goes off.

His father told him that once when he was his son's age he had been tempted to shoot at birds, and had one day shot a blackbird out of an apple tree. But this gun was not a powerful one, and he found that he had wounded the bird horribly. It laid at his feet struggling and gasping, and he had looked down on it in horror, sickened by what he had done and not knowing what to do next. Because of the shame of this misdeed, he told his son not to shoot at birds, not just because his gun was insufficiently powerful, but because no civilised man shoots a bird he does not intend to eat, just as he never shoots a man unless at war. He said 'You must promise me never to shoot a bird you do not intend to eat, nor ever to shoot another man unless you are at war. Do you promise?'

'Yes, father, I promise.'

'If I catch you shooting birds, I will take your gun away and keep it until you have a son to whom I can give it.'

In every little boy there is a hunter and a warrior, and every human being is fascinated by violence. Accordingly, this little boy was tempted by his father's words. He stalked a sparrow in a hedge, and shot it. He watched it die in the grass, the blood pearling out of its beak in scarlet drops, and then wondered what to do with the corpse. He picked it up and felt the softness of its feathers then its diminishing warmth. Tears welled up in his eyes, and hastily he gave the bird to the family cat, because then at least it would have been eaten and he would not have entirely betrayed his promise to his father. Guilt struck him to the heart and he climbed a yew tree in order to be alone. He sat in the fork of the trunk and felt his face glowing with the shame.
It was three years later that he found a young jackdaw with a broken wing, hopping and circling on the grass of the lawn. He took it indoors and showed it to his father, who said 'Do you want me to kill it? It may be the most merciful.'

'No,' said the boy. 'I want us to cure it.' He had it in his mind that he owed a debt to the birds, and this was how the debt might be repaid. Because his father had been a soldier, he knew how to make a splint, so accordingly he found two thin strips of wood and some narrow bandage. Whilst the boy held the terrified and confused bird as still as he could, his father clipped the quills from the wing, and carefully but firmly bound the broken limb. 'There' he said, 'we've done our best, and now
it's down to nature and good luck.'

The boy fed the bird on cat food, grapes, and worms. Because the bird was very young, it was easy to tame, and soon it was sitting on his shoulder, investigating his hair and ears, murmuring quietly, and leaving long streaks down the back of his shirt. He made a perch for it in his bedroom, with newspaper on the carpet underneath, and in the mornings the jackdaw awoke him by declaring its hunger and its eagerness for the new day's life.

Because the bird was young, its bones healed quickly, and thanks to the splint, there was only a small knob of bone under the shin where the ends had grown back together. But feathers take a very long time to grow, and first of all the stubs of the old ones had to grow out and be shed, and so the boy kept the bird for mort

In every little boy there is a hunter and a warrior, and every human being is fascinated by violence. Accordingly, this little boy was tempted by his father's words. He stalked a sparrow in a hedge, and shot it. He watched it die in the grass, the blood pearling out of its beak in scarlet drops, and then wondered what to do with the corpse. He picked it up and felt the softness of its feathers then its diminishing warmth. Tears welled up in his eyes, and hastily he gave the bird to the family cat, because then at least it would have been eaten and he would not have entirely betrayed his promise to his father. Guilt struck him to the heart and he climbed a yew tree in order to be alone. He sat in the fork of the trunk and felt his face glowing with the shame. It was three years later that he found a young jackdaw with a broken wing, hopping and circling on the grass of the lawn. He took it indoors and showed it to his father, who said 'Do you want me to kill it? It may be the most merciful.'

'No,' said the boy. 'I want us to cure it.' He had it in his mind that he owed a debt to the birds, and this was how the debt might be repaid. Because his father had been a soldier, he knew how to make a splint, so accordingly he found two thin strips of wood and some narrow bandage. Whilst the boy held the terrified and confused bird as still as he could, his father clipped the quills from the wing, and carefully but firmly bound the broken limb. 'There' he said, 'we've done our best, and now
it's down to nature and good luck.'

The boy fed the bird on cat food, grapes, and worms. Because the bird was very young, it was easy to tame, and soon it was sitting on his shoulder, investigating his hair and ears, murmuring quietly, and leaving long streaks down the back of his shirt. He made a perch for it in his bedroom, with newspaper on the carpet underneath, and in the mornings the jackdaw awoke him by declaring its hunger and its eagerness for the new day's life.

Because the bird was young, its bones healed quickly, and thanks to the splint, there was only a small knob of bone under the shin where the ends had grown back together. But feathers take a very long time to grow, and first of all the stubs of the old ones had to grow out and be shed, and so the boy kept the bird for more than a year.

One day his father said to him 'Did you know that dinosaurs are not extinct after all? We were all completely wrong. They are beginning to think that the little dinosaurs survived, so now we have lizards and amphibians, and birds. Just imagine! It turns out that some of the dinosaurs had beaks and feathers. Isn't that a miracle? We look out of our windows and see the trees full of little dinosaurs!'

That evening the boy sat his jackdaw on its perch and looked into its face. He recognised the extreme antiquity of its being, and said to it 'Your soul is millions of years more ancient than mine. My soul is young compared to yours.' The bird looked back into his eyes and shook its wings a little, just as a fledgling does when hoping to be fed. The boy stroked the back of its neck and the bird blinked. 'We are so different,' thought the boy, 'and yet there is affection and understanding.'

When at last the jackdaw had regrown its feathers, the boy's father said 'Now you must teach the bird to fly.'

'But it might fly away.'

'Yes, it might, and if it does, it might come back or it might not. You must understand that
birds are not like us. The essence of man is to be a prisoner, but the essence of a bird is to

be free. A bird shows no passport at the borders. It pays no taxes. A bird has no pockets and when it dies it has no shroud. The nearest it has to money is when it hides its food from other birds. The reason birds sing
than a year.

One day his father said to him 'Did you know that dinosaurs are not extinct after all? We were all completely wrong. They are beginning to think that the little dinosaurs survived, so now we have lizards and amphibians, and birds. Just imagine! It turns out that some of the dinosaurs had beaks and feathers. Isn't that a miracle? We look out of our windows and see the trees full of little dinosaurs!'

That evening the boy sat his jackdaw on its perch and looked into its face. He recognised the extreme antiquity of its being, and said to it 'Your soul is millions of years more ancient than mine. My soul is young compared to yours.' The bird looked back into his eyes and shook its wings a little, just as a fledgling does when hoping to be fed. The boy stroked the back of its neck and the bird blinked. 'We are so different,' thought the boy, 'and yet there is affection and understanding.'

When at last the jackdaw had regrown its feathers, the boy's father said 'Now you must teach the bird to fly.'

'But it might fly away.'

'Yes, it might, and if it does, it might come back or it might not. You must understand that birds are not like us. The essence of man is to be a prisoner, but the essence of a bird is to be free. A bird shows no passport at the borders. It pays no taxes. A bird has no pockets and when it dies it has no shroud. The nearest it has to money is when it hides its food from other birds. The reason birds sing is because they like to have something enjoyable to do with their free time, and the reason that they fly in high winds is just for the fun of it. They have the fre dom of the air. We have two legs, just like the birds, but because we have no wings we are prisoners of the earth. For us the birds represent all the freedom we can never have. They give us something to aspire to that we cannot reach. And sometimes when you aspire to what you cannot reach, one day after all, you reach it.' That evening the boy repeated to the bird on its perch in his bedroom 'Your soul is more ancient than mine.'

Louis de Bernières,
Author

A FRAGILE GLASS LANDING – A HOPE FOR WINGS TO GROW

Prof. Dr. Stefan Weber
Director, Museum of Islamic Art, Pergamon Museum

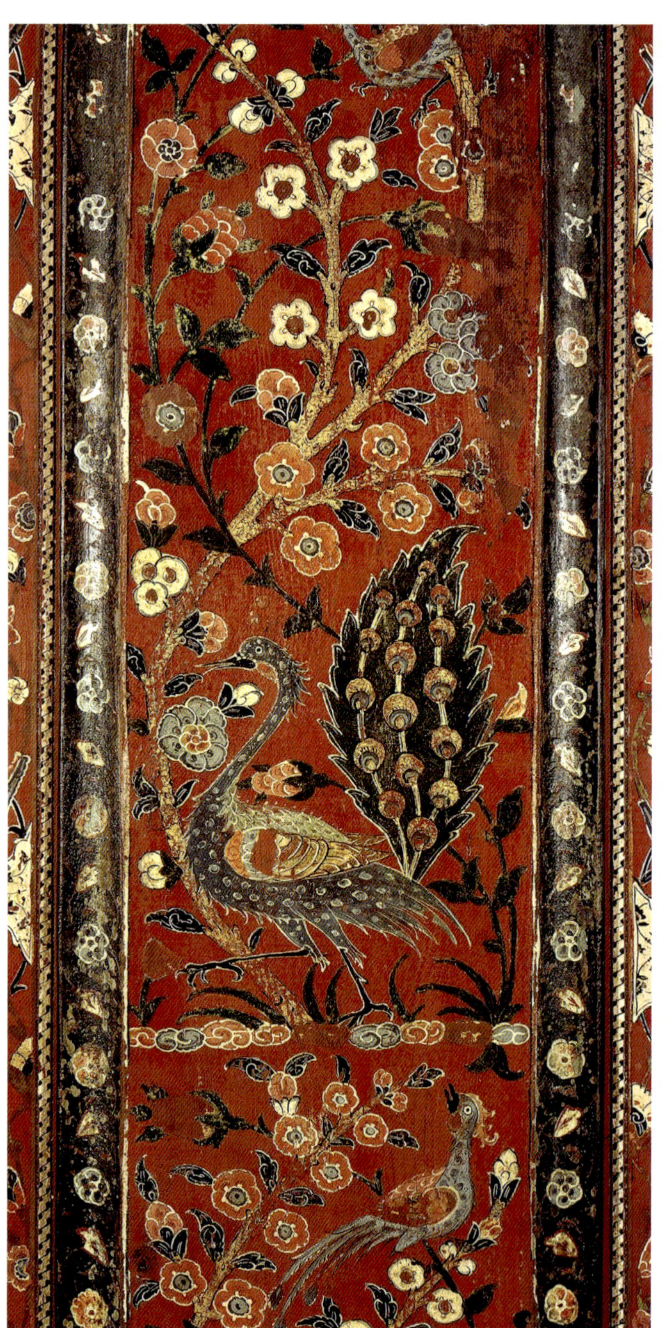

They sit in small groups, picking at the ground next to each other seemingly peacefully. At first glance they appear charming, small and delicate. In January 2018, 27 glass swallows by artist Felekşan Onar moved into the Aleppo Room of the Museum of Islamic Art for a three-month stay. At first glance they appear gentle and delicate, but, in fact, they portray a humane catastrophe of our times. The installation is the artist's attempt to raise awareness for the situation of Syrian refugees in her hometown of Istanbul. According to the UN refugee organization UNHCR, there were 4.1 million refugees and asylum seekers worldwide in 2019, with over 3.6 million Syrian refugees in Turkey. More than 500,000 Syrians are supposedly living in Istanbul. The Museum of Islamic Art has been linked with Turkey and Syria for decades, and we feel directly affected by this situation. So what have we been doing to resolve it?

Our responsibilities to Syria have manifested themselves in a masterpiece of the museum – the spectacular, colourfully painted wooden panelling from the Wakil House in Aleppo. The Aleppo Room once embellished a prestigious reception room in the Syrian city. The splendid wooden panels were commissioned from 1600–03 by the

Detail from the Aleppo Room.
Photo: Johannes Kramer
© Museum of Islamic Art / Pergamon Museum

View of the installation *Perched*
at the Pergamon Museum.
Photo: David von Becker
© Museum of Islamic Art / Pergamon Museum

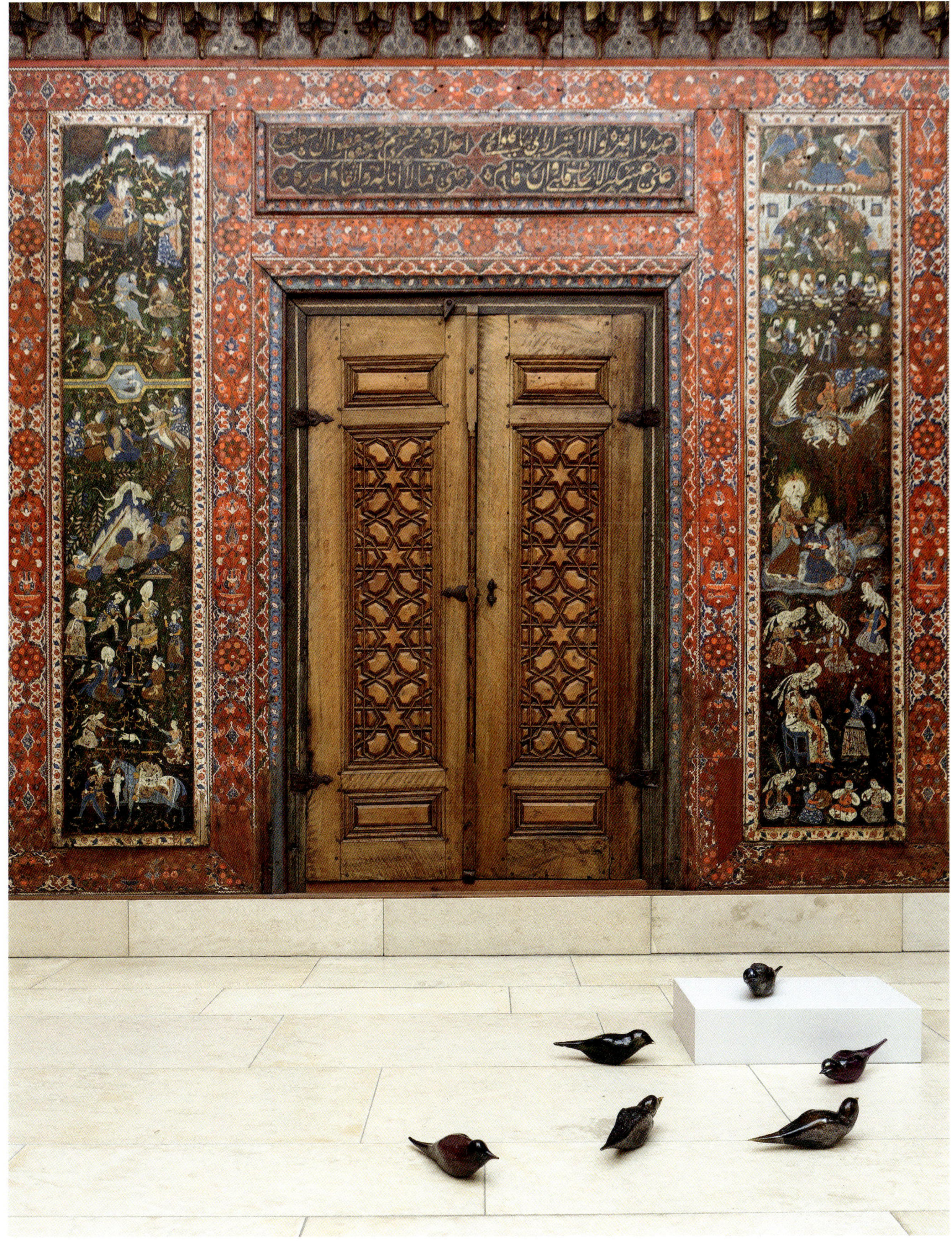

owner of the house, the Christian merchant Isa ibn Butrus, and most likely crafted by Persian artists. In 1912, the director of the Museum of Islamic Art, Friedrich Sarre, purchased the panelling from the then residents of the house. At that time, dozens of old wall panel sets were being sold or disposed of in order to make room for new decorative elements. The panels in Berlin are also unique in terms of their subject-matter: the magnificent décor, the numerous figural depictions of religious and profane subjects as well as the craftsmanship demonstrate a cosmopolitan and tolerant city life in Aleppo during this period. For decades, the museum has been studying the architectural and artistic past of Syria – evidence of multi-ethnic and multi-religious cohabitation. And the swallows from Istanbul recall precisely these elements.

Felekşan Onar's 2017 installation of 27 form-blown glass swallows ties directly into the ornamental décor of the Aleppo Room. The lively, colorful peacocks, ducks and pigeons on the wall panels stand in almost oppressive contrast to the small, fragile birds with clipped wings seated on the ground. Not only does the installation resonate with the sad fate of a once flourishing metropolis – now destroyed by the civil war – but it also picks up on the reality of Syrian refugees in modern Turkey. Onar was inspired to her intervention by the scenes she witnessed in the vicinity of her atelier in Istanbul's Pera district. "The stranded refugees find themselves in the middle of a chaotic city. They sit on steps and pedestrian paths, not knowing what will happen next or where they must go …. They are making a stopover here, but aren't capable of flying or even moving." The small birds have no wings. These are not happily twittering, fluttering birds in the courtyard of the Wakil House in Aleppo, but small, fragile birds with cropped wings on the ground. The aim of this contemporary intervention is not only to reflect on the situation in Istanbul, but also to transmit it to the world of the visitors.

Many people also came to Germany from Aleppo and Syria, not only to stop over, but, in the end, to stay. Museums have a specific responsibility to think and act globally. We are part of a giant worldwide archive, which documents, studies and preserves global cultural heritage, and we can and must react to various global challenges. The Berlin

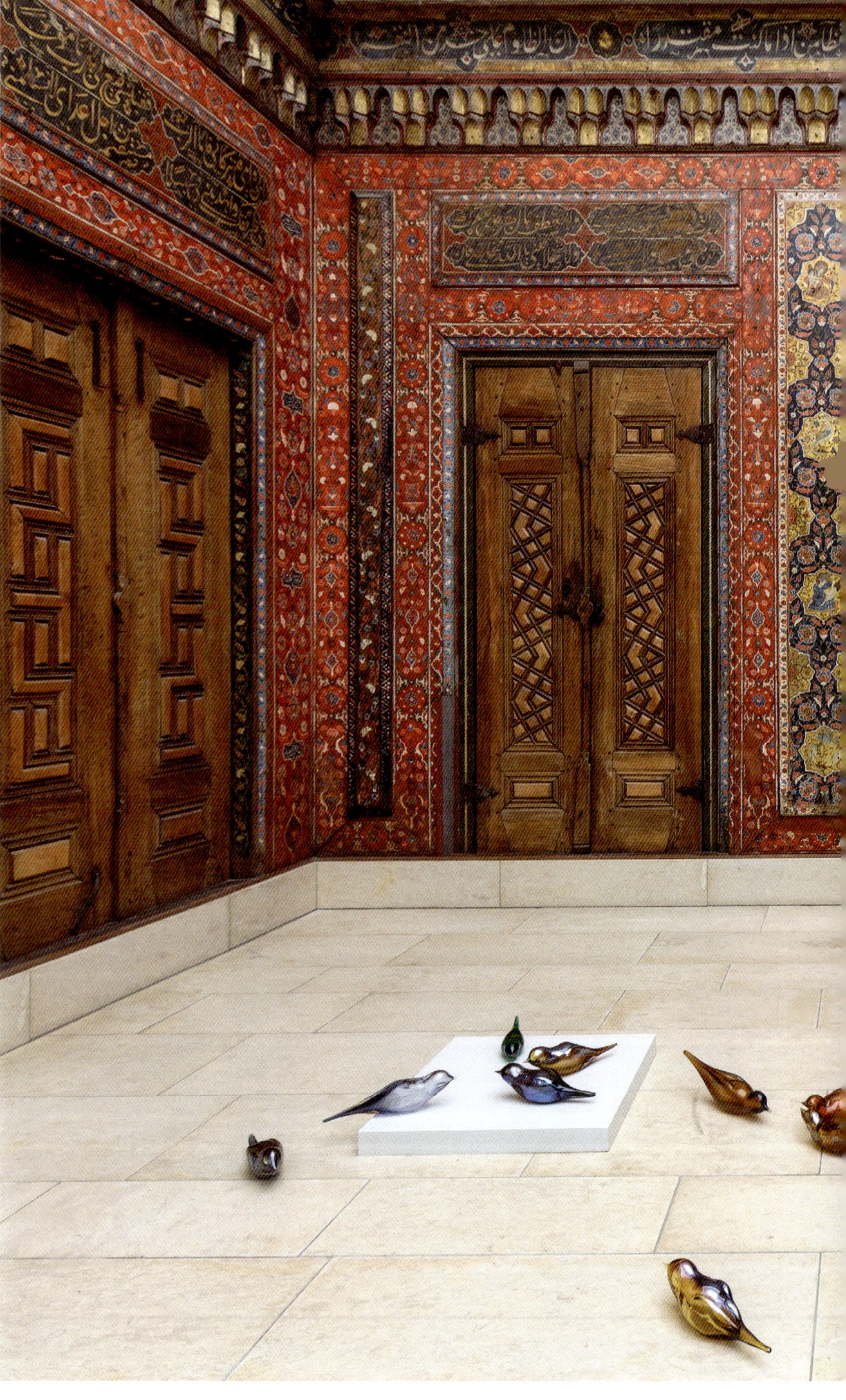

View of the installation *Perched*
at the Pergamon Museum.
Photo: David von Becker
© Museum of Islamic Art / Pergamon Museum

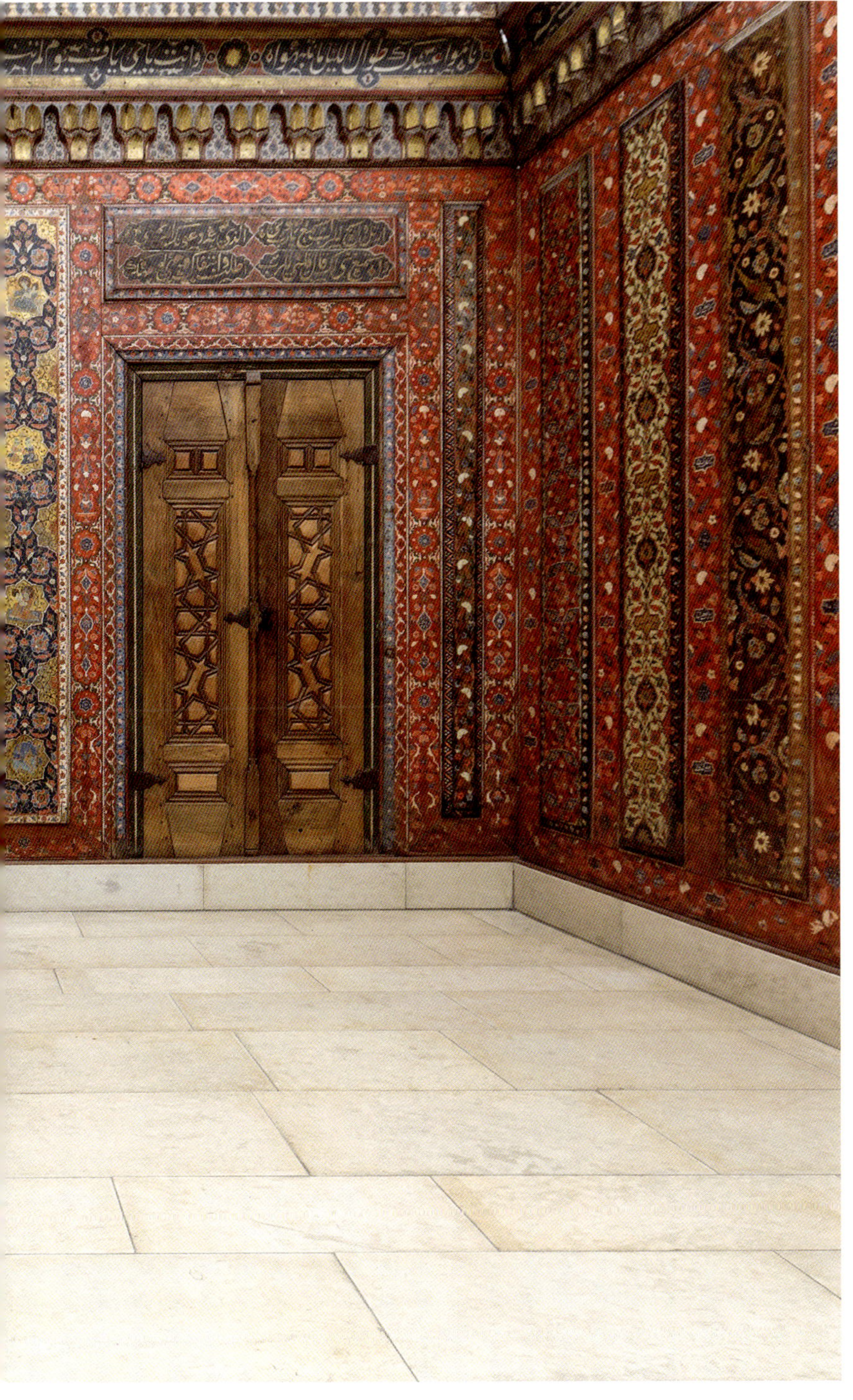

Multaka project, *Museum as a Meeting Point – Refugees as Guides in Berlin Museums,* trains Syrian and Iraqi refugees as museum guides to offer museum tours for Arabic-speaking refugees in their native language. Multaka (Arabic: meeting point) stands for the exchange of diverse cultural and historical experiences. At present, the project is running in over a dozen museums with over 100 guides and ten thousand visitors who have experienced flight. The museum can help them to land and truly arrive, and thus expand the traditional borders of public institutions serving a society in transformation.

More importantly, many of those who arrive here can grow their wings! We keep witnessing inspiring life stories within Multaka. For example, we have over ten specialists from Syria – architects, monument conservators and art historians – helping the museum develop the archives, make them accessible for the reconstruction and communicate with the Syrian community about cultural heritage. The archives are being expanded in a mutual effort to include perspectives from the community. Aleppo is particularly important for us, and we are documenting entire city districts, their historical significance, the destruction and the memories – in the hope that the swallows will once again fly over the rooftops of the city with ease. Museums can recognize their historical responsibility, and this can contribute to the shaping of our society. In 2018, the jury of the Museum & Heritage Awards in London concluded that Multaka is 'Impressive and timely, it not only protects the heritage and history of Syria but reminds us of our global responsibility'.

The works of Felekşan Onar were created in April 2017 in the atelier of the Berlin Glassworks, which belongs to our dear friend Nadania Idriss. The installation was her idea. Miriam Kühn and Martina Kopp brought the idea to reality. We are grateful to all of them! The exhibition included the video project *The Aleppo-Room* by Polish artist Viktor Witkowski. He accompanied four refugee guides from the Multaka team, who, amongst other things, offer tours in the Pergamon Museum. They describe their personal thoughts about their favourite objects, including the Aleppo Room.

I hope that Felekşan Onar's swallows will sensitize and inspire many visitors!

PERCHED:
AN INSTALLATION REFLECTING ON THE SYRIAN REFUGEE CRISIS

Mariam Rosser-Owen
Curator, Victoria and Albert Museum, London

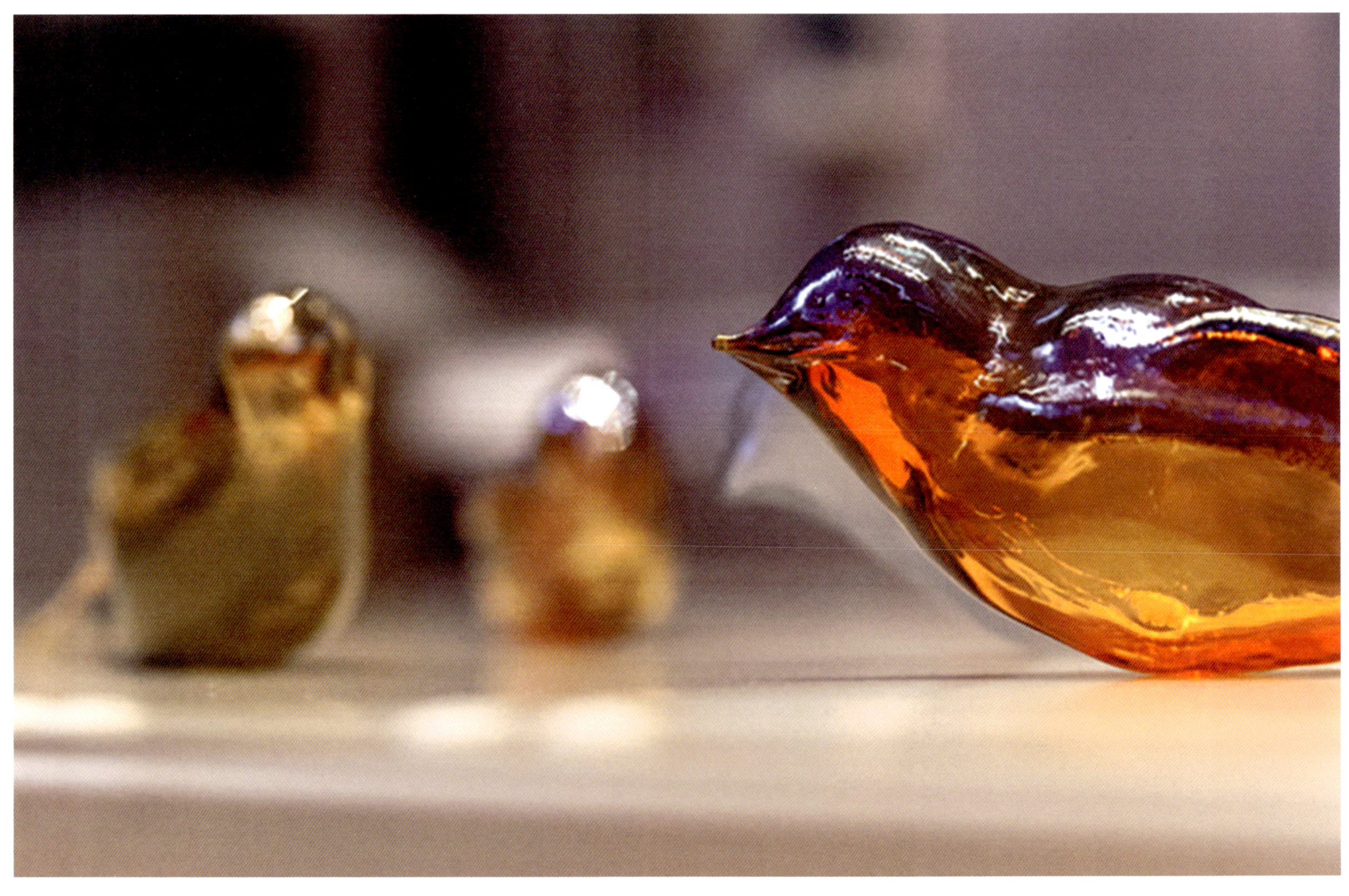

Perched was an installation in the V&A's Islamic Middle East Gallery from 16 June 2018 to 22 April 2019. It comprised a flock of 41 mould-blown glass swallows, made by an artist and designer from Turkey, Felekşan Onar. Apart from interventions during Jameel Prize 2011, this was the first time we had shown contemporary art by a Middle Eastern artist in the gallery.

The swallows have trimmed wings and are unable to fly. They are Onar's artistic response to the millions of displaced Syrians in Turkey. Having fled a war, many of these refugees have landed in Istanbul, where Onar lives. Like the birds in *Perched*, they are unable to move on. They are grounded, with nowhere else to go.

The inspiration for the swallows' form came from *Birds Without Wings*, the historical novel by Louis de Bernières. The novel is set during the wars between Greece and Turkey in the early 20th century, as the Ottoman empire broke up. The fighting caused millions to abandon their homes: Christians fled to Greece, Muslims to Turkey. Finally, in 1923, an official exchange of populations was agreed, forcing migration on those who had not yet fled. Onar remembers stories of this time from her childhood. She talked movingly about her inspiration for the display in an interview for *Hyperallergic*.

Numbers are significant to Onar. Though she is not superstitious, her work is firmly embedded in Turkish cultural traditions. She explains that almost every day a Turkish person says "41 times masha'Allah", one more than 40, to invoke good fortune and keep away the evil eye. Traditionally in Turkey, when you invite neighbours to a feast, the custom is to make 41 different dishes. 40 is an important, holy number in many religions, so one more than 40 makes extra good luck. Onar has been making her art pieces in repetitions of 41 – for example, the installation of glass bridges *41X* combining Venetian and Ottoman architectural forms,

at Venice Glass Week in September 2018 – so that when she had to decide how many birds to make, 41 was the first number that came to her mind.

Onar started working with glass in 2003 and uses various techniques to showcase the qualities of the material. She says, "Through glass, I speak, breathe and live". The birds in *Perched* were made at Berlin Glassworks, where Onar had a residency. She started by sculpting a swallow from clay, which became the master model from which to make a two-piece plaster mould. The glass birds were blown into the mould, using each mould about 6–8 times before it fell apart.

The two parts of the mould were opened to release the bird, which was still hot from the furnace, allowing the artist to sculpt the tail or make changes to the posture – tilting the head, raising the body, etc. This means that each bird is unique. The bird's tail remained attached to the blowing rod until the bird was finished; that area was then cold-worked, using mechanical tools and machines to polish it and flatten a small area where the bird can sit. The artist also etched in her signature and the number of that bird within the wider group.

The birds are all different colours and some of them have a beautiful lustre to them; others have a surface effect that looks like feathers. To achieve this effect, Onar used coloured glass granules made of pulverized glass with metal added to make the colours. She sifted these on to the glass surface while it was still hot, sometimes in the form of larger granules, sometimes more of a powder, resulting in different surface textures. The lustre effect happens when elements in the colour, such as iron or copper, are hit with a flame from the furnace or a torch; this causes a reduction in the elements and they become metallic. It's a bit like the raku process in ceramics – they are burned after firing in order to give them a metallic surface effect.

We knew the birds were different colours before they arrived, but nothing prepared us for how colourful they actually were when we started to unpack them and see them all massed together for the first time. To start with, I grouped them by colour and then went on to work out what might

Perched at the V&A.
Photo: Daniel Oduntan
© Victoria and Albert Museum

be sub-groupings within the wider group of 41: which colours and poses would work well together. Felekşan had seen photographs of the display case and the glass shelves reminded her of the telephone wires that real-life swallows perch on; she thought that at least half of the birds should sit on the shelves. That was the only steer she gave me in terms of how the birds should be displayed. I looked at pictures of swallows online to give me ideas for how they could be grouped, and this inspired me to show some side by side, others next to each other but facing in different directions. We were reusing a tall narrow plinth from the previous display that had been in that case, which invited the notion of birds drinking water at a fountain, so I selected two whose beaks pointed downwards. One of the birds had a particularly downward tilting head, which invited the slightly cheeky notion of it peering down on you from above. But I was also conscious that these birds represented refugees so there should be a sense of distance and isolation, even while they were loosely grouped together.

The display opened in time for Refugee Week in June 2018 and even became the lead image on the event leaflet and website. We also organized a really moving evening event for V&A Members, in which Felekşan Onar came together for the first time with Louis de Bernières, whose book had so inspired her. They each talked individually about their own works, followed by a discussion and questions from the audience. Louis de Bernières shared the hope that *Birds Without Wings* would be the book he was remembered for. A reception followed as well as a book signing – copies of the book literally flew off the shelves.

In October we organized that Felekşan should give an *In Focus* talk in front of the display, which was extremely well attended – more people turned out to hear her than often come for these talks, including students from Imperial College, over the road, who (I was amazed to hear) were writing about *Perched* for their studies. Since then I have met an art history MA student who had chosen to write about *Perched* for his dissertation.

With a display like this, which is open to anyone visiting the Museum, it can be difficult to gauge the

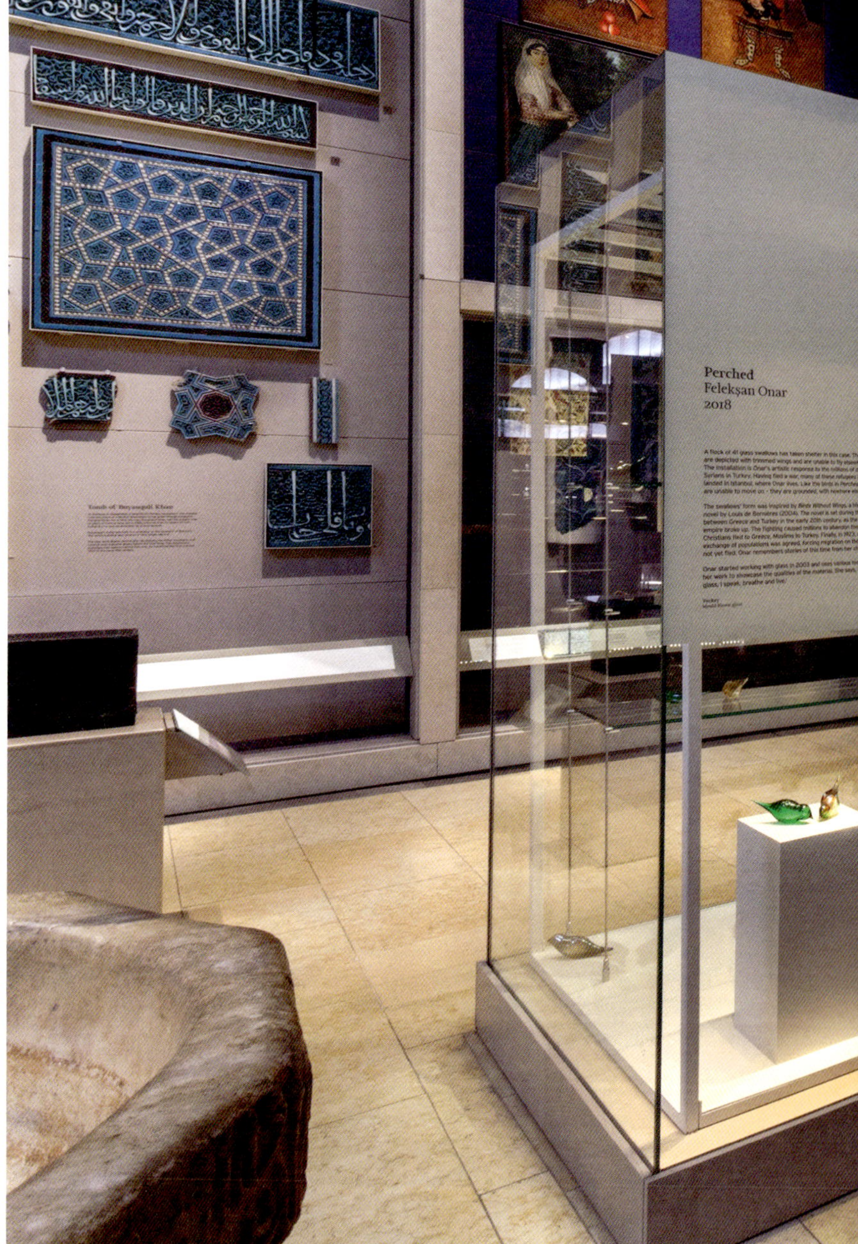

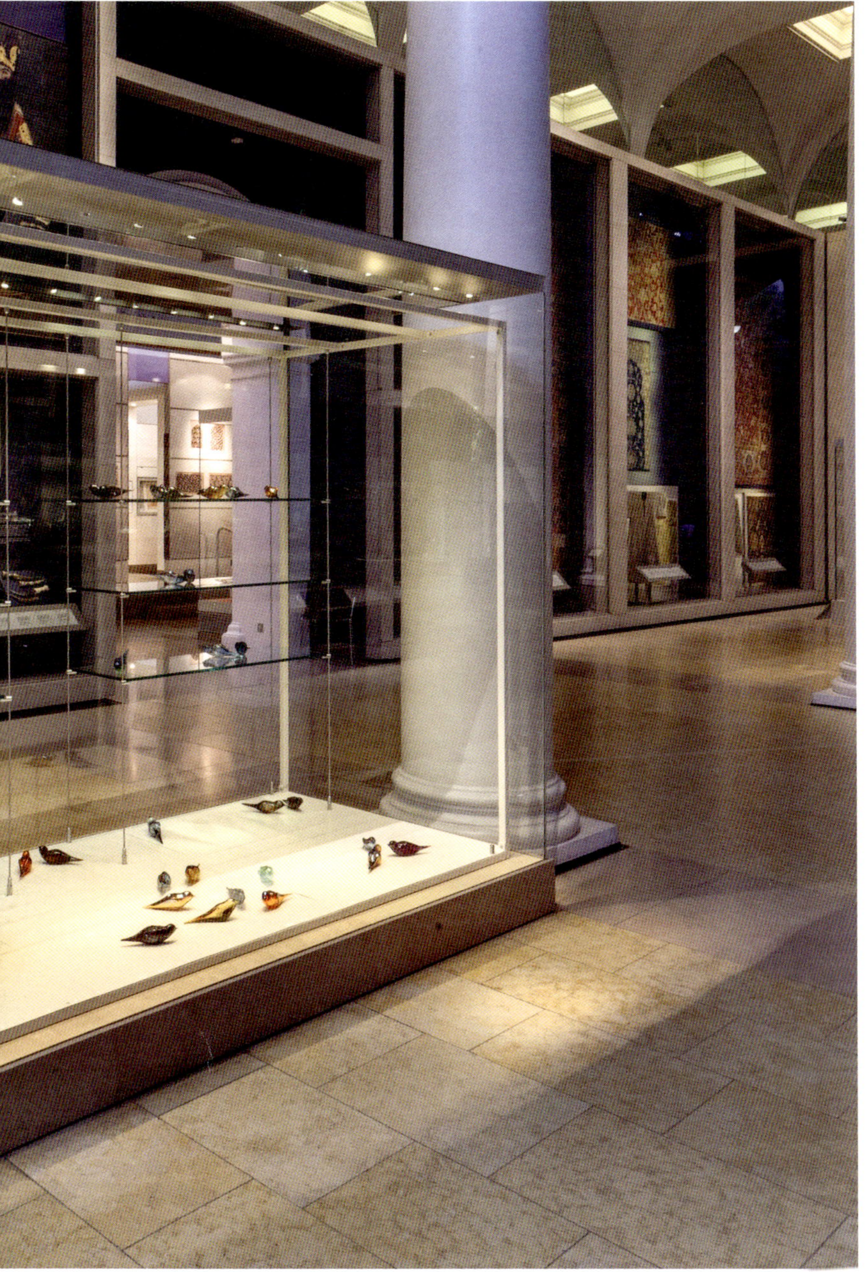

View of the installation *Perched* at the V&A.
Photo: Daniel Oduntan
© Victoria and Albert Museum

reaction of visitors, but this installation seems to have attracted a lot of attention. People were drawn towards the case by the delicate beauty of the birds, then they read about its meaning and were deeply moved. Even while we were installing the display, a group of school children wandered over and looked at the birds. I saw people sitting and drawing in front of the case. I was told that the Museum's guides included the display on their introductory tours, and one of them passed on this message: "It's an incredibly moving work; I always get a really positive and sympathetic response to it when I include it in my Intro tours".

Other visitors have shared their comments on social media: @peterkeyngaert commented on Instagram that *Perched* was "probably the most beautiful and touching work currently at @vamuseum …. You cannot see this and remain unmoved by the tragedy so many people face".

When the display closed here at the end of April 2019, the birds flew back to their temporary home in Berlin. Onar has now raised the total number of the birds in the flock to 99, another significant number in Muslim cultures, as Allah has 99 names or attributes. Onar has been looking for other venues for the birds to fly to – especially in the West, where she feels the refugees' story still needs to be heard – though we are delighted that seven of the birds have remained in the V&A and have been accessioned into our permanent collection (ME.15 to 21-2019). Seven – again a significant number for Felekşan: she says it is "one of the most magical and holy numbers throughout history and across cultures". Onar talks about how a group of seven swallows feels to her "like a community", so that a display on a much smaller scale than we currently have in the Jameel Gallery can still convey her original message. It was our pleasure to provide a safe haven to the larger flock for nearly a year, and we hope this little community will soon find a permanent home in the V&A's Glass Gallery.

A FRAGILE FEELING:
Conversation with Felekşan Onar

Glenn Adamson
Curator, writer

In May 2020, with us both under lockdown conditions due to the coronavirus pandemic, I had the pleasure to interview Felekşan Onar over Zoom; though we were 5000 miles apart, we had a warm and intimate conversation about her upbringing, business career, her turn to art, and the ideas that led her to create *Perched*. An edited transcript follows.

Felekşan Onar: I grew up in a traditional farming town - at the time, it took four hours to get to Izmir by car. My grandfather farmed cotton, my father had gone into setting up production facilities for fabric – the next step. I attended a missionary boarding school, set up by Americans, and I was quite passionate to do well. I was also exposed to glass-painting there, and I loved it, but the reason I did it was to refresh my mind so I could study better in math and physics; it was a way for me to do better academically, which I thought was the thing to do.

I was the only person from my school who went to study in the U.S., at Cornell, where I studied economics. Right after graduation I was hired by Citibank, which I thought would give me a good perspective on Turkish industry. I wanted to set up my own businesses, which I have done together with husband: we've employed as many as two thousand people producing jeans wear. By the year 2000, though I was still very young, I was in several business associations, dealing with social and political issues: Turkey joining the EU, Turkish women gaining a better standing in the business world, setting up peace forums between Turks and Greeks. These were the things on my agenda. However, I was extremely frustrated. In these types of associations, you get nowhere; often, you are the only one who does any work.

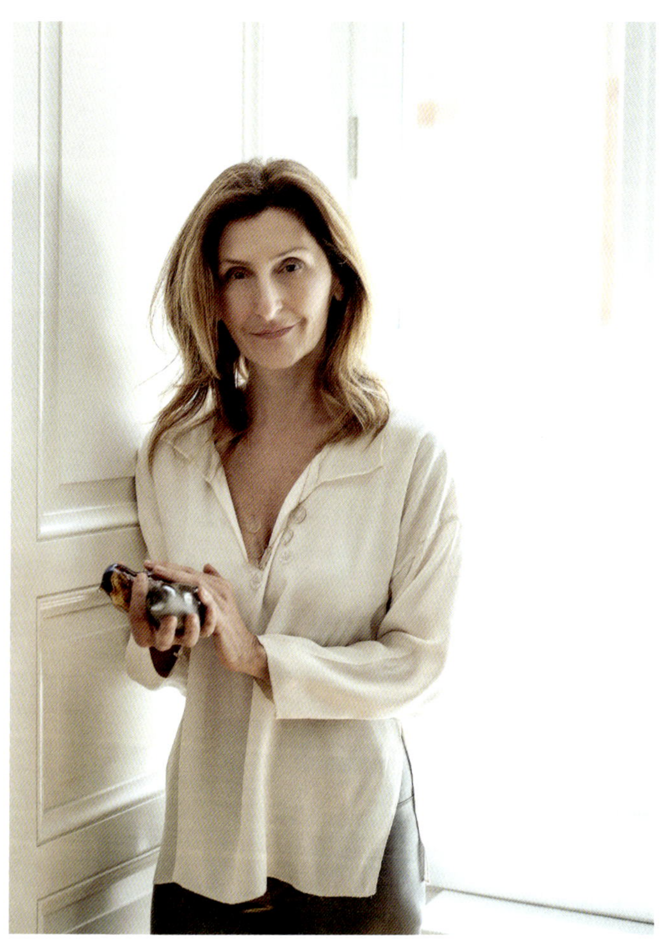

Felekşan Onar
Photo: Serkan Eldeleklioğlu

So I said to myself, maybe it's time for me to refresh my studies. I already had a family, so the best way to do it was to get a business executive education, which I did at Harvard, from 2000 to 2003. I was one of the youngest among 120 people there, and I realized the issues they were dealing with weren't changing with experience and age. My frustrations would not get any better, if I stayed in the business world. So I came back home, and I told my husband – can you imagine, just back from Harvard? – "I don't want to be in a management position anymore. I am just done." And at that point I really did not know what to do next. Probably for the only time in my life.

Glenn Adamson: *Did you find this turning point exciting? Or terrifying?*

FO: Neither. I was happy to be able to sit with that decision; what I had already done in business was enough. Now I could just contemplate and spend time with my children, who were still very young at the time. Then, only two or three months into my 'sabbatical', I found myself drawing glass objects. To start with, large sculptural bowls.

GA: *So you were thinking of yourself as a designer, rather than a maker?*

FO: Exactly. But coming from a production background, I told myself: it makes no sense to draw something when you don't know how it will be produced. You must go out and learn how glass is produced. This was 2003. I thought glass could be made in only one technique, this is how naïve I was. Having already taken so much time away from my family, though, I could not just go to the U.S and study glass. So my only option was to look into what is possible in Turkey. I found this atelier in Istanbul that was teaching hobby glass techniques, mainly fusing. The very first time I went, I realized that designing something and letting someone else make it was not what I wanted to do. Because with glass, you can alter it throughout the process. So I formulated a curriculum for myself: fusing, casting, blowing, cutting, etc. Six months into this, a world-class school called the Glass Furnace opened in Istanbul: a turning point in my career. Dale Chihuly came to teach there, Lino Tagliapietra. That first year I studied with a French artist, Chantal Royant, who taught me kiln-casting.

GA: *When you made this shift into being a maker, did you realize what a learning curve you had in front of you?*

FO: Yes. I was very conscious: you have to remember, I was producing 50,000 pairs of jeans one day, and the next day I was producing only one object at a time. My friends would say, "Felekşan, what are you doing, are you wasting your life?" Or, "I cannot wait to see the thousands of plates you will make for export." But that is not where I wanted to go, because if you make thousands of something, it doesn't matter if it's glass or a pair of pants. I wanted to stay in the craft, do it with my own hands.

GA: *Can you talk about the stylistic approaches you took in this early work? I feel that you are not that insistent on pursuing a specifically Turkish style; I think of Art Nouveau in some of the forms, for example.*

FO: I wanted first to test the boundaries of the material, that is where I started. Since I do not come from a fine arts background, it was not going to be very detailed; but I realized I could express myself with glass. The forms, colours, would explain the story of where I come from: my experience as a woman in Turkey; my heritage. I also spend a lot of time with nature, that is where I get the colour stories.

What put me on the path I am on today, though, is the exhibition I did with a Syrian calligrapher, Mohammed Imad, in 2015. This was the time when we started getting Syrian refugees into Turkey, and he was a neuroscientist who had to flee with his family; now he makes a living by writing the Quran. Unbelievable. He writes a Kufi script, which is very geometrical and architectural. This attracted my attention, and I thought: I should stop running away from my heritage, I should go back and use it in a way that suits me. We had an exhibition together where I used calligraphy in my glass, and I made spinning bowls – an Eastern form. From then on, I started reflecting my background in glass. And I realized the frustration I'd had as a businesswoman did not exist for me as an artist.

GA: *I have been to Istanbul only once, but I know there is a strong debate between modern secular tendencies and opposing tendencies that are more nationalistic and religious.*

FO: Turkey is a land where people of many different backgrounds have been able to live and learn from each other. This is where I get my strength. I am open to other cultures, I am adaptive, I learn languages. I think this character is not only specific to me but to many Turks. I want to show this to the world. When I was young, if there was a visitor to Istanbul I would have them visit a mosque, a church and a synagogue, all within 300 meters. This is what I try to explain in my stories. For example, a project I am doing in Venice is building glass bridges; the Ottoman Turks traded glass in the Mediterranean starting in the thirteenth century, and today as a glass artist I am invited to Murano. The material itself is a bridge between cultures.

GA: *So you don't really have to choose between local tradition and the global, because Istanbul has been the crossroads of the world for so long.*

FO: Exactly. Where I was brought up in the western part of Anatolia is a mix of Greek and Turkish culture. When I moved to Istanbul – I was 25 or so – some of the words I used didn't exist here. They were Greek words, but growing up I thought they were Turkish.

GA: *Let's talk about Perched, and the development of that project.*

FO: 2016 is when the real flood of Syrian refugees came, and in July, we had the attempted coup. The globalized citizens of Turkey felt: what if we cannot leave? What if it becomes like Iran here? What if women lose their rights? I felt like I had to get out of Istanbul, and start practising elsewhere. Maybe one day I would have to do it anyway.

So I went to Berlin, a city that accepted a population of Turkish immigrants decades ago, and I am thinking, will I be one of those one day? And I was walking around Berlin, bumping into the Turkish families who have been there since the 1960s, but it is as if they have just arrived. Seeing them reminded me of the Syrian refugees that we had in Istanbul. What I saw in their eyes was the same: not knowing what they are doing there, and what is next for them.

GA: *So the bird is an image of provisionality.*

FO: Yes. Neither the Syrian nor the Turkish immigrants would sit comfortably; they would lean against a wall, or sit on the pavement – momentarily. This took me back to a book I read many years ago, *Birds Without Wings* by Louis de Bernières. Once I remembered it I knew the form I wanted to use; I walked into the glass studio and said, "guys, this is what we are going to do: make birds with closed wings." And also, I wanted to use a new technique. I wanted something of my hand in this. I made birds out of clay, and then took plaster molds, and the team blew glass into these molds. This gives a very fragile feeling; unlike any technique I have used before.

The owner of the glass workshop is old friends with the director of the Islamic Department in the Pergamon Museum. As soon as she realized what I was up to, she called him and asked him to visit. So even while we were blowing, I already knew that if successful, it would be shown in the Aleppo Room at the Pergamon Museum. This doesn't happen to an artist very often.

GA: *How did you feel when you saw the birds in the galleries?*

FO: It brought tears to my eyes, it really did. The context is so important: the minute the visitors walk in, they already know they are in the Middle East. I placed the birds on the floor, not on pedestals, so they are vulnerable; so even without reading the story they are able to know what this is about. A conservator at the museum told me that she had worked there for 25 years, and the Aleppo Room never attracted this kind of attention before.

And then I was connected to Miriam Rosser-Owen at the V&A. There, we placed the majority of the birds on glass shelves, which makes them look as if they are sitting on wires, as birds do. We contacted Louis de Bernières, who lives nearby London, and we had a talk together at the museum. The next destination for the birds will be in Dresden, at the Stadtmuseum – in the Damascus Room that has not been reconstructed since its donation to the museum in early 1930s.

GA: *Birds are migratory, and unaware of national boundaries. Do you think of the flock of birds as a transnational image, in some way?*

FO: I do want to make them free. If they want to open their wings, they can fly; it is only themselves, keeping themselves stuck like that. I am hoping that, next, we will bring them to North America. The birds' migration will be across the northern hemisphere, like a lot of immigrants who end up in North America. As the story unfolds, I would like their final settling to be there. A peaceful last stop.

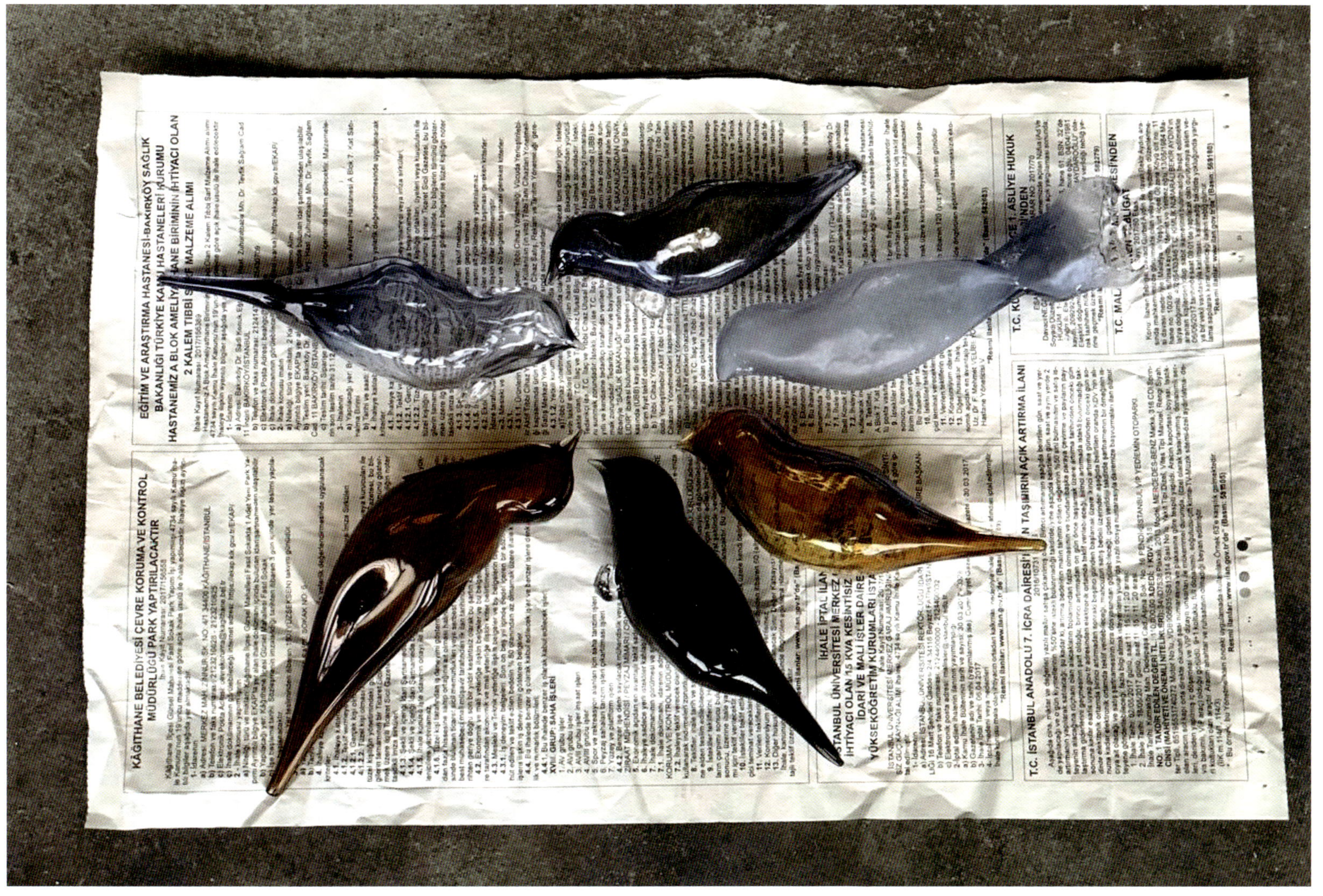

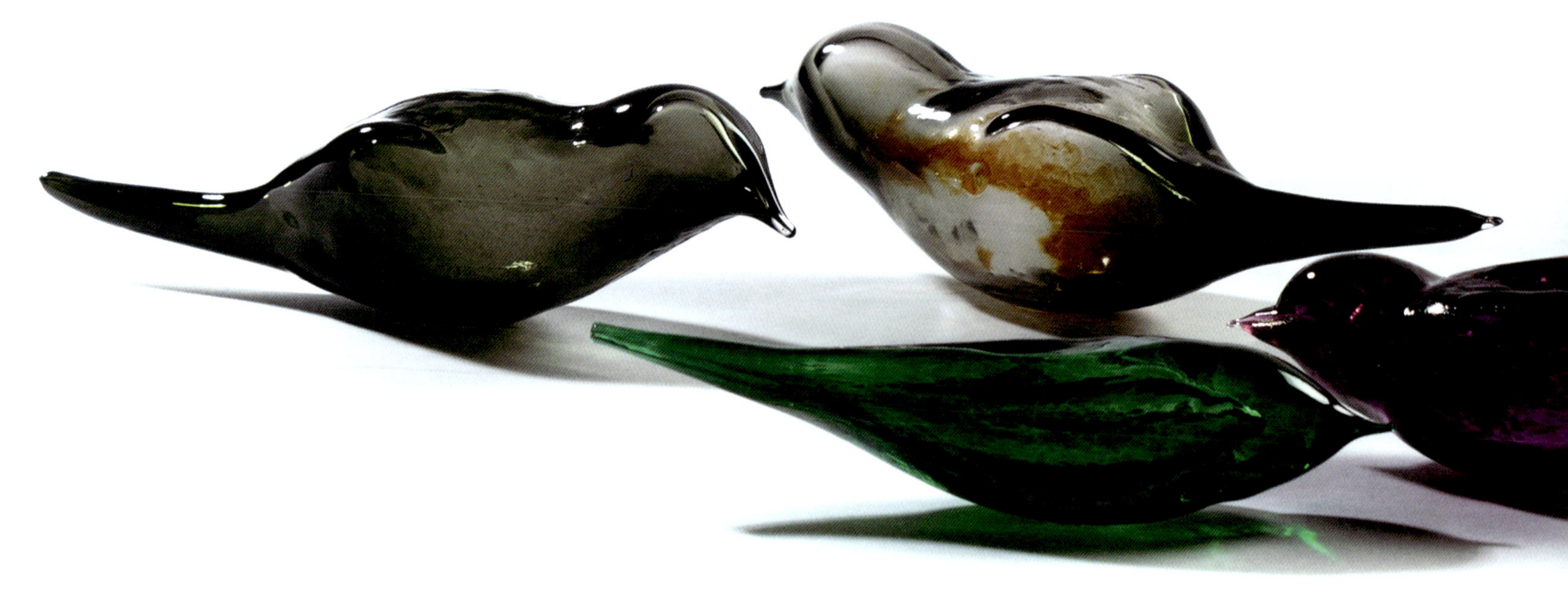

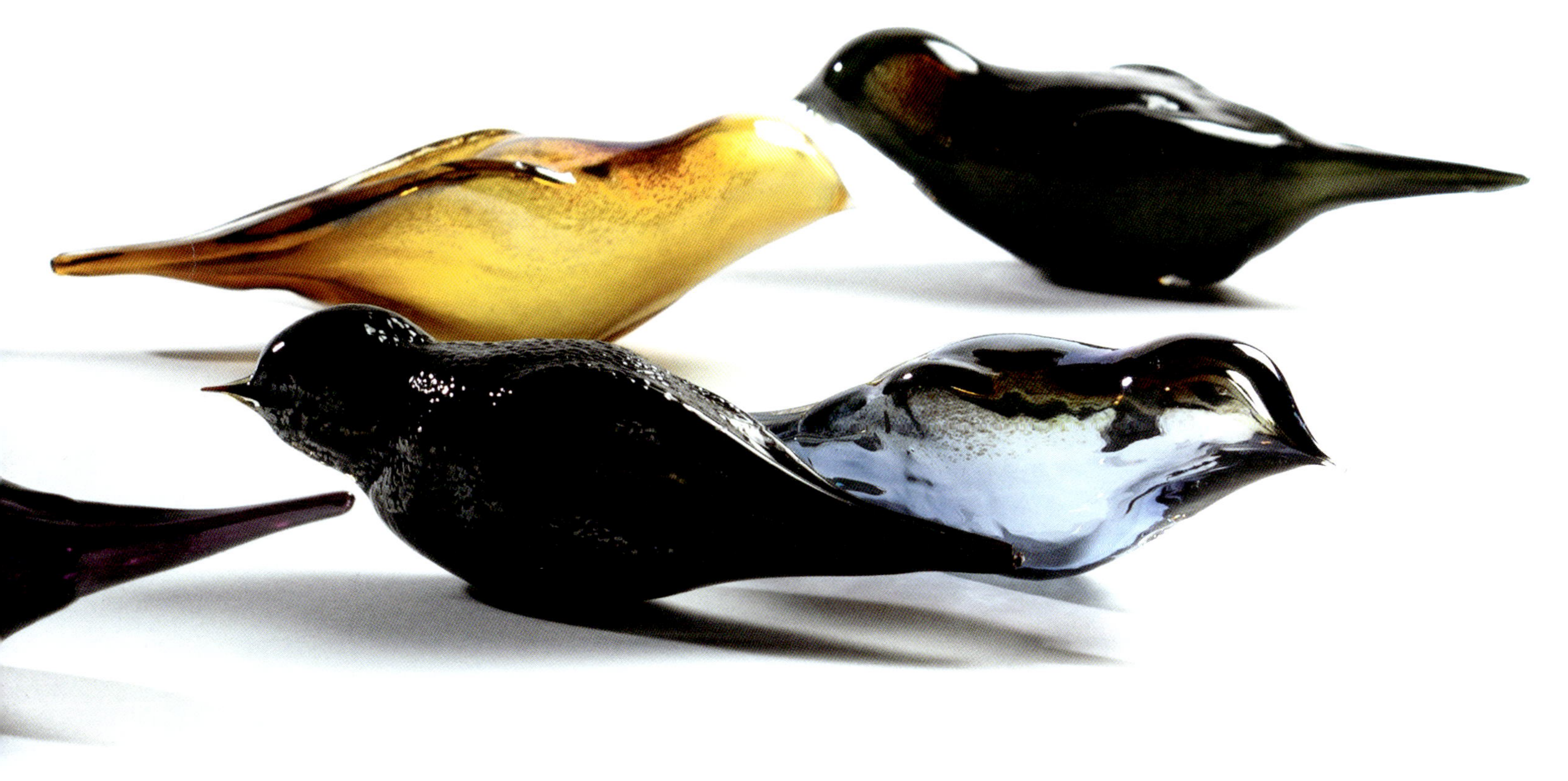

34

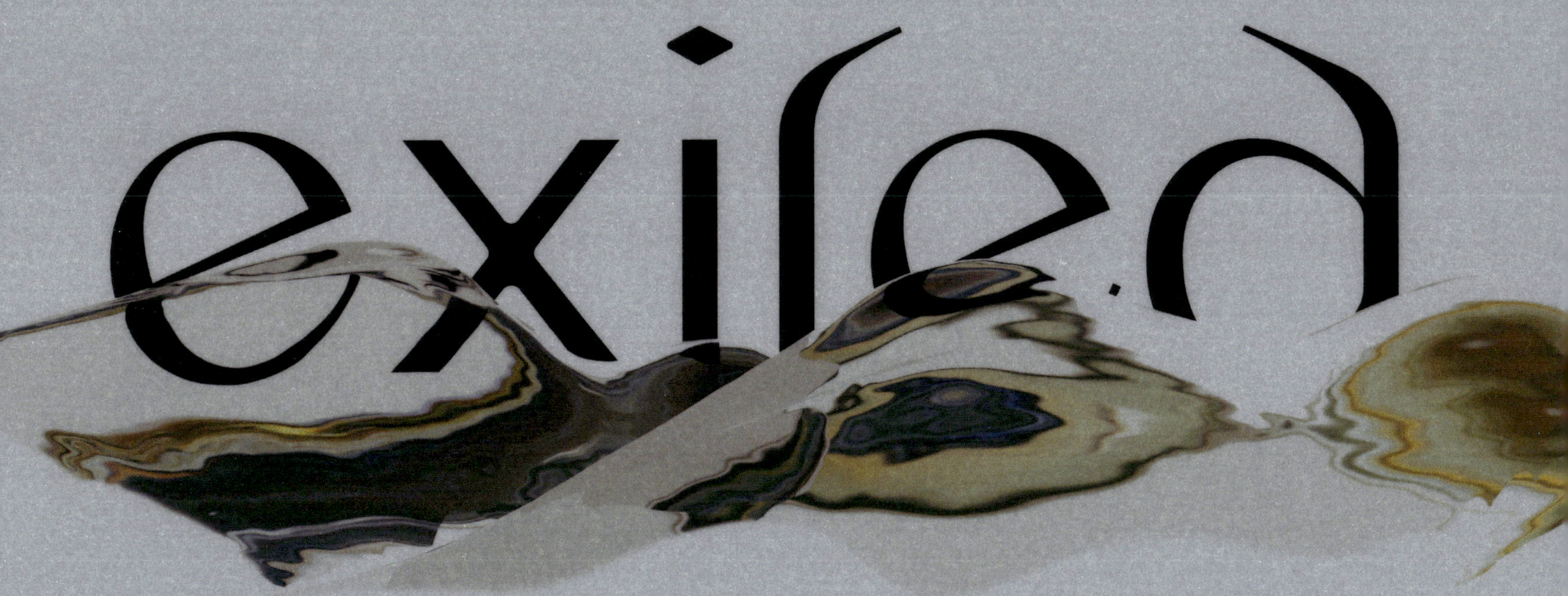
exiled

helixe

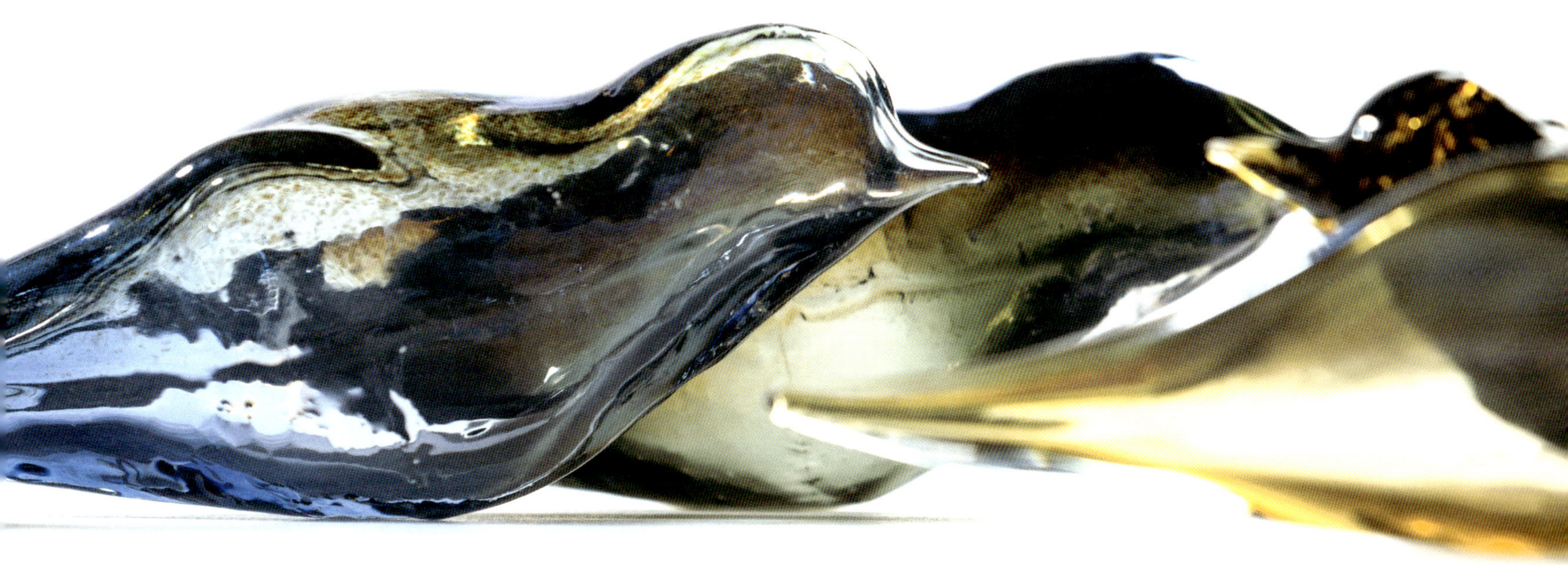

Perched Photos: Dario J. Laganà

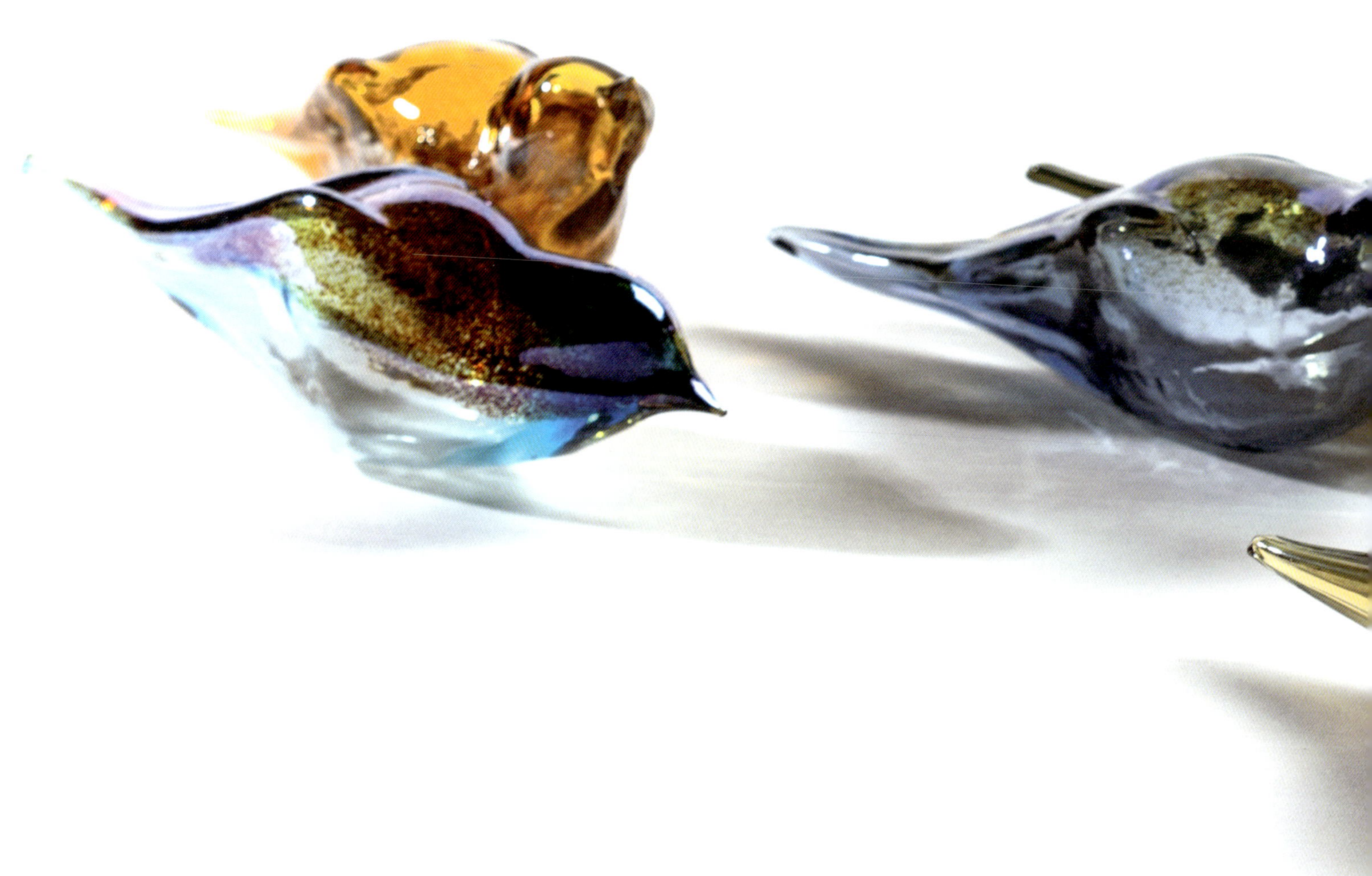

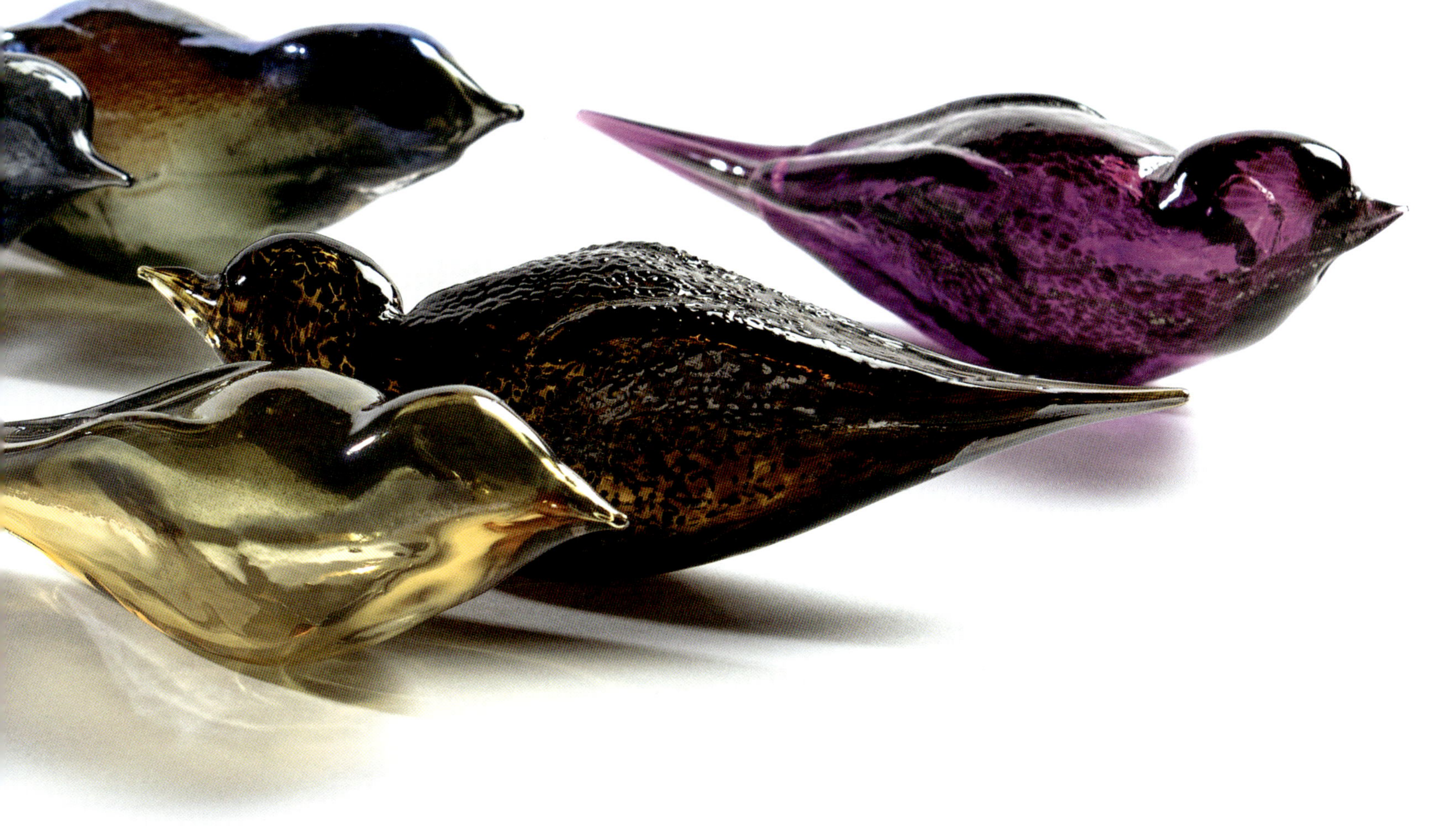

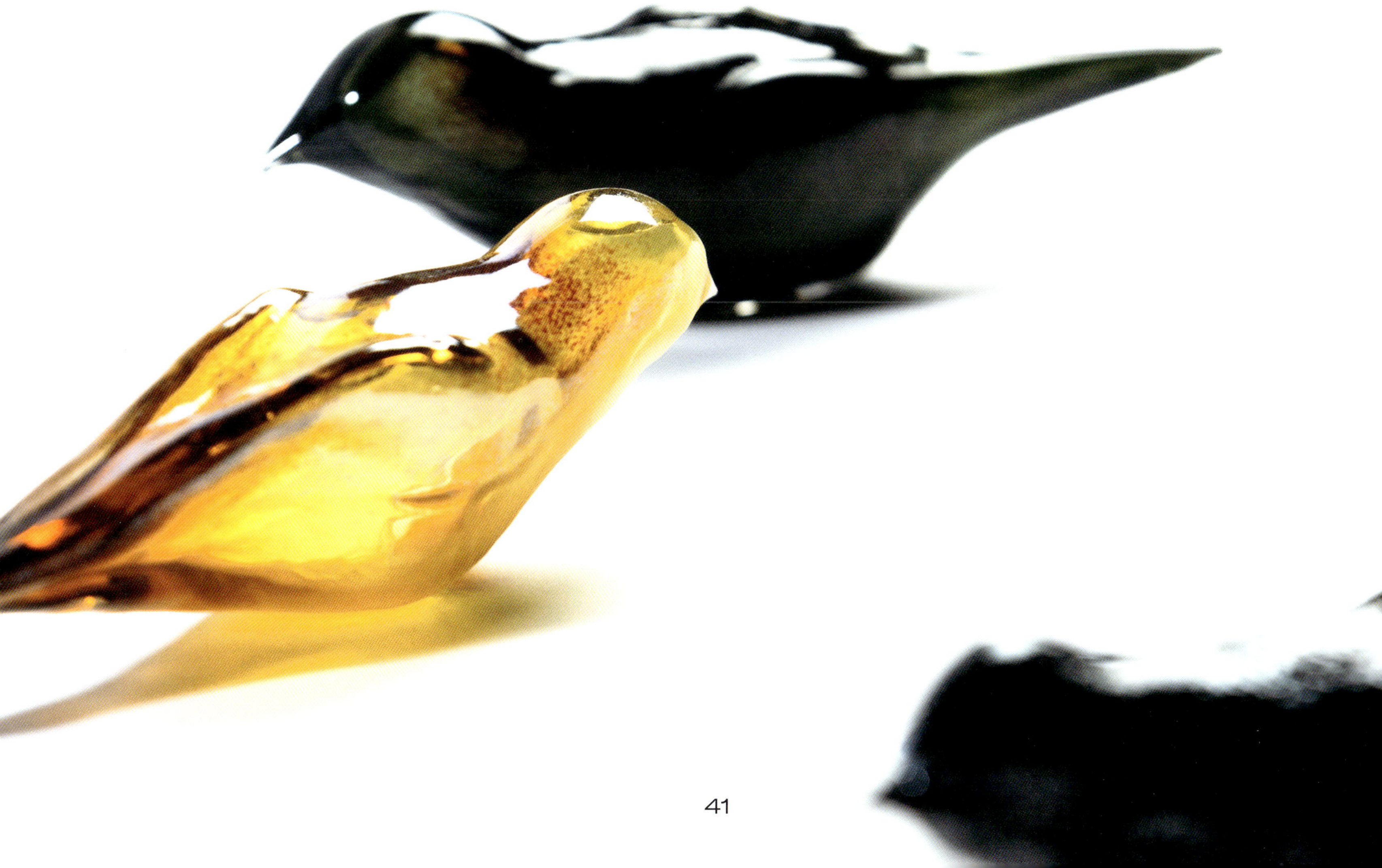

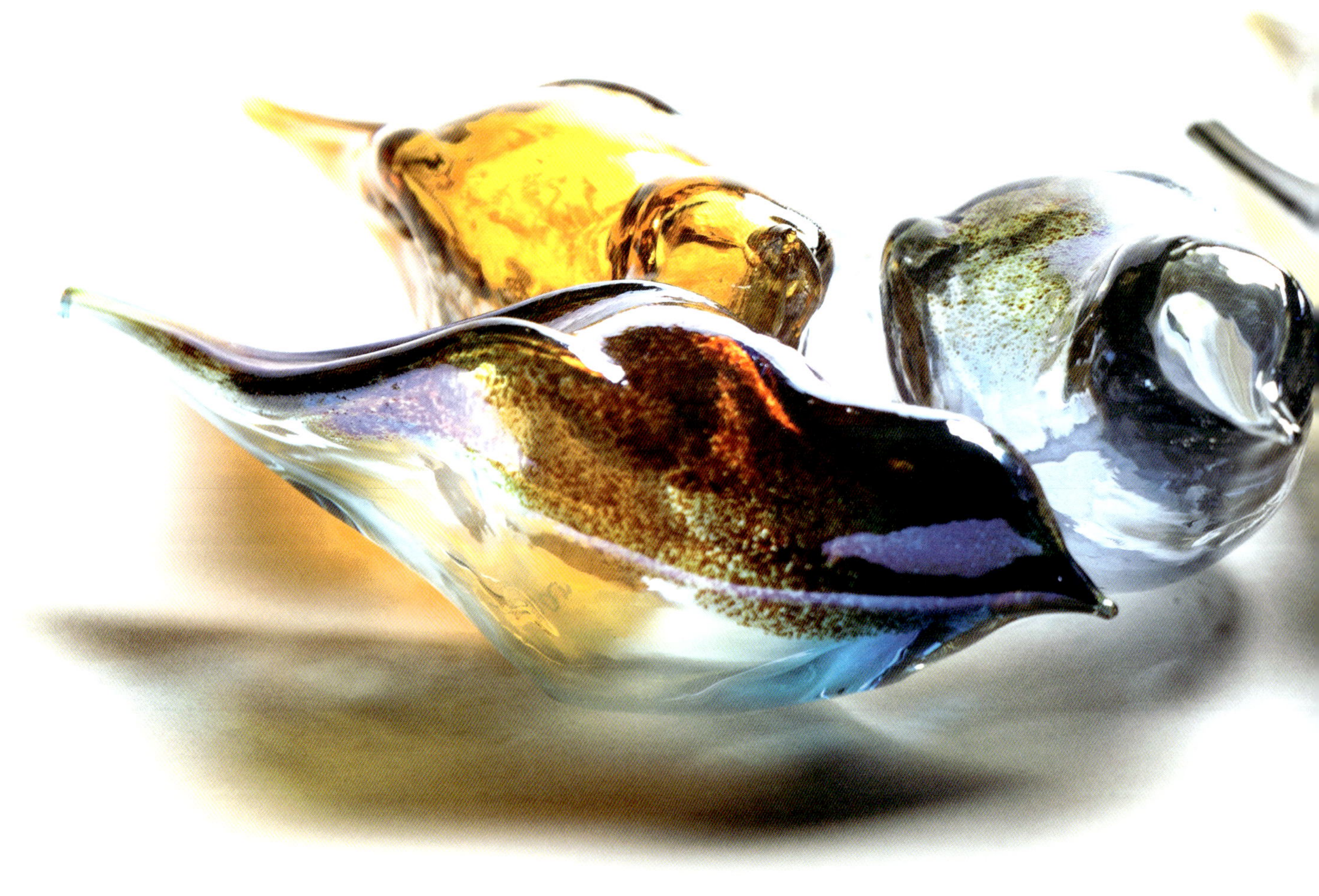

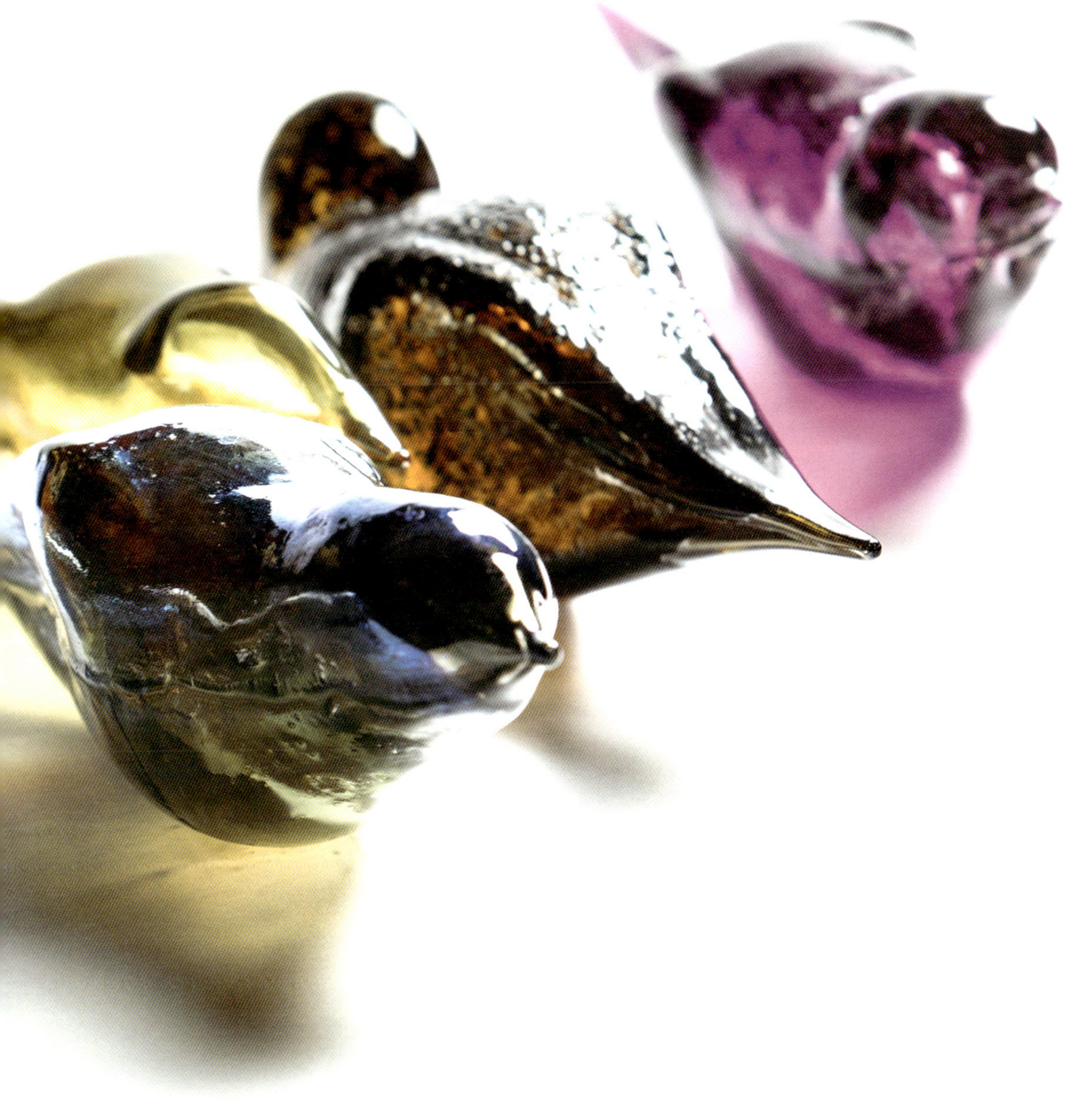

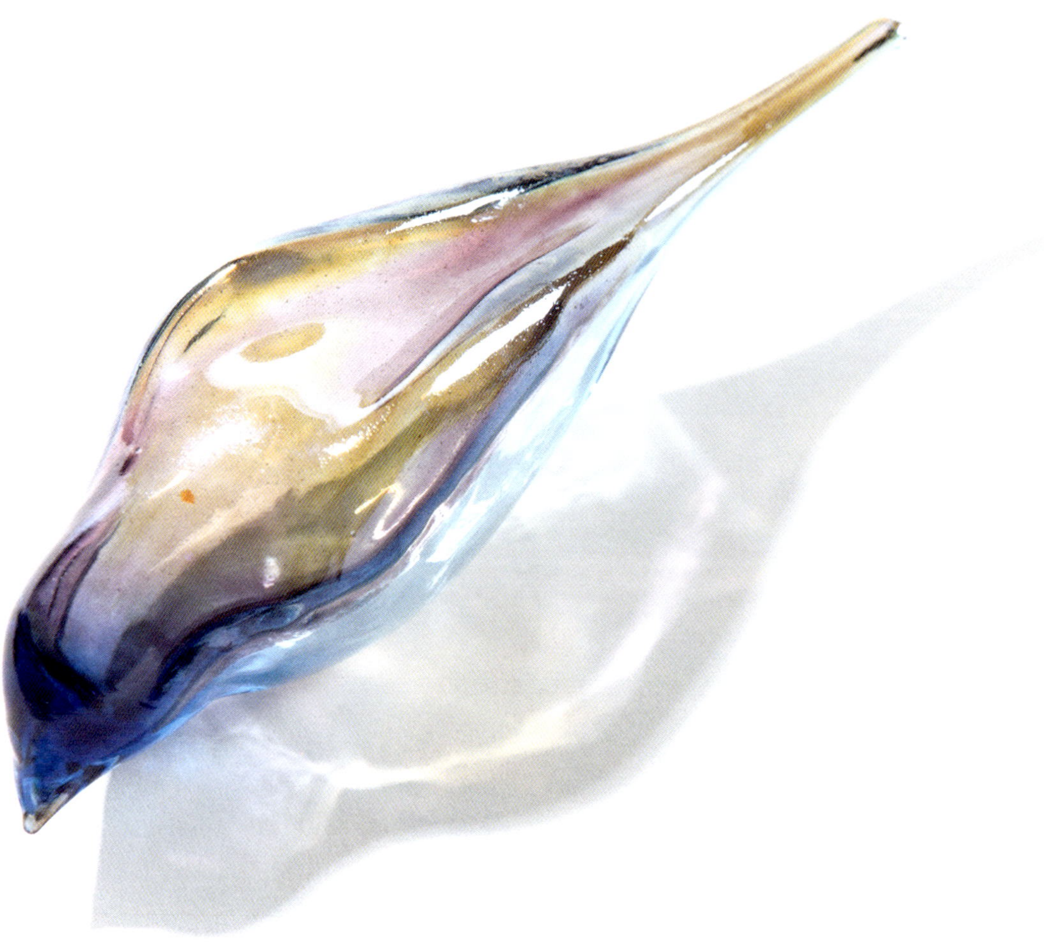

distanced

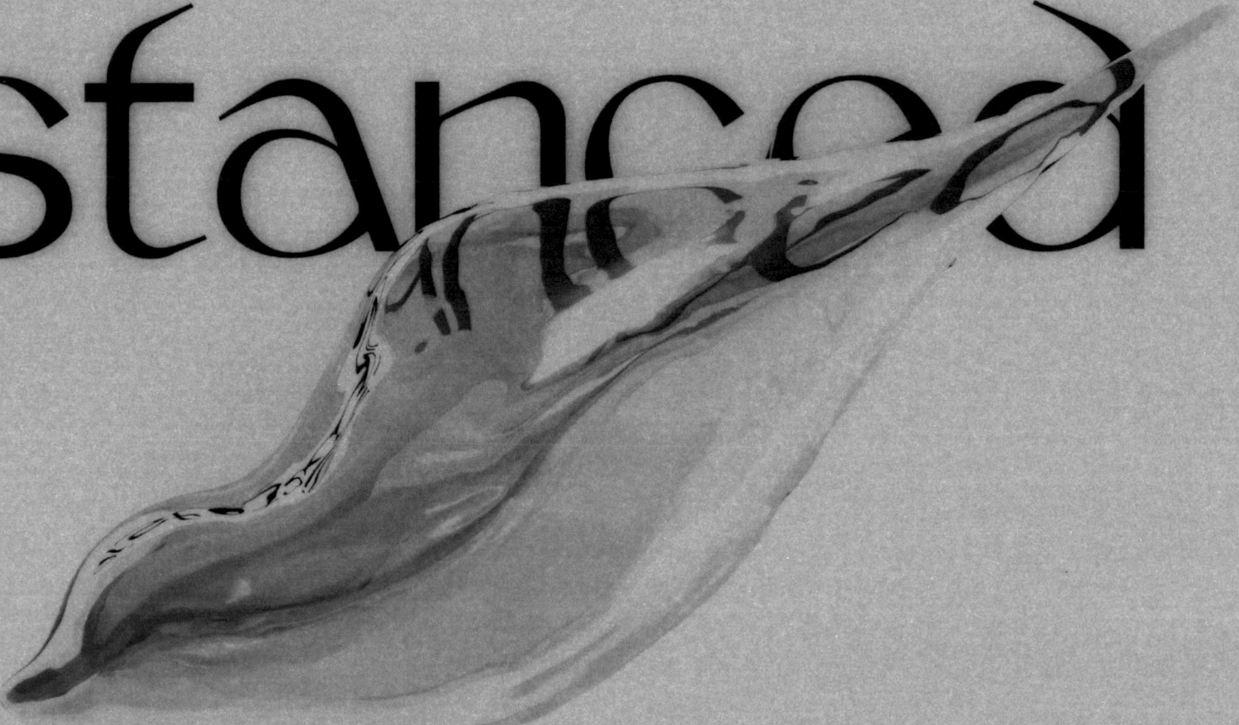

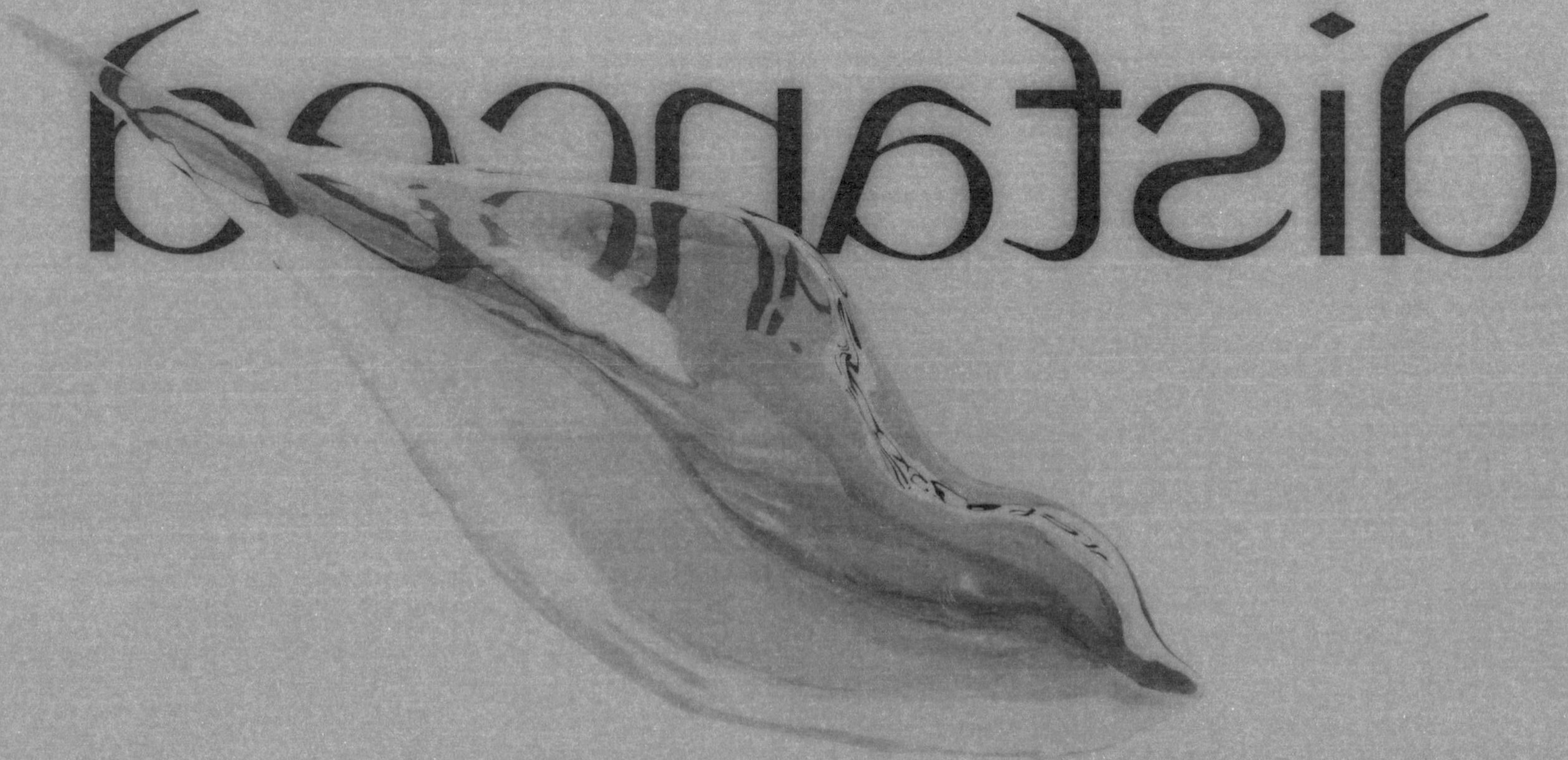

distanced

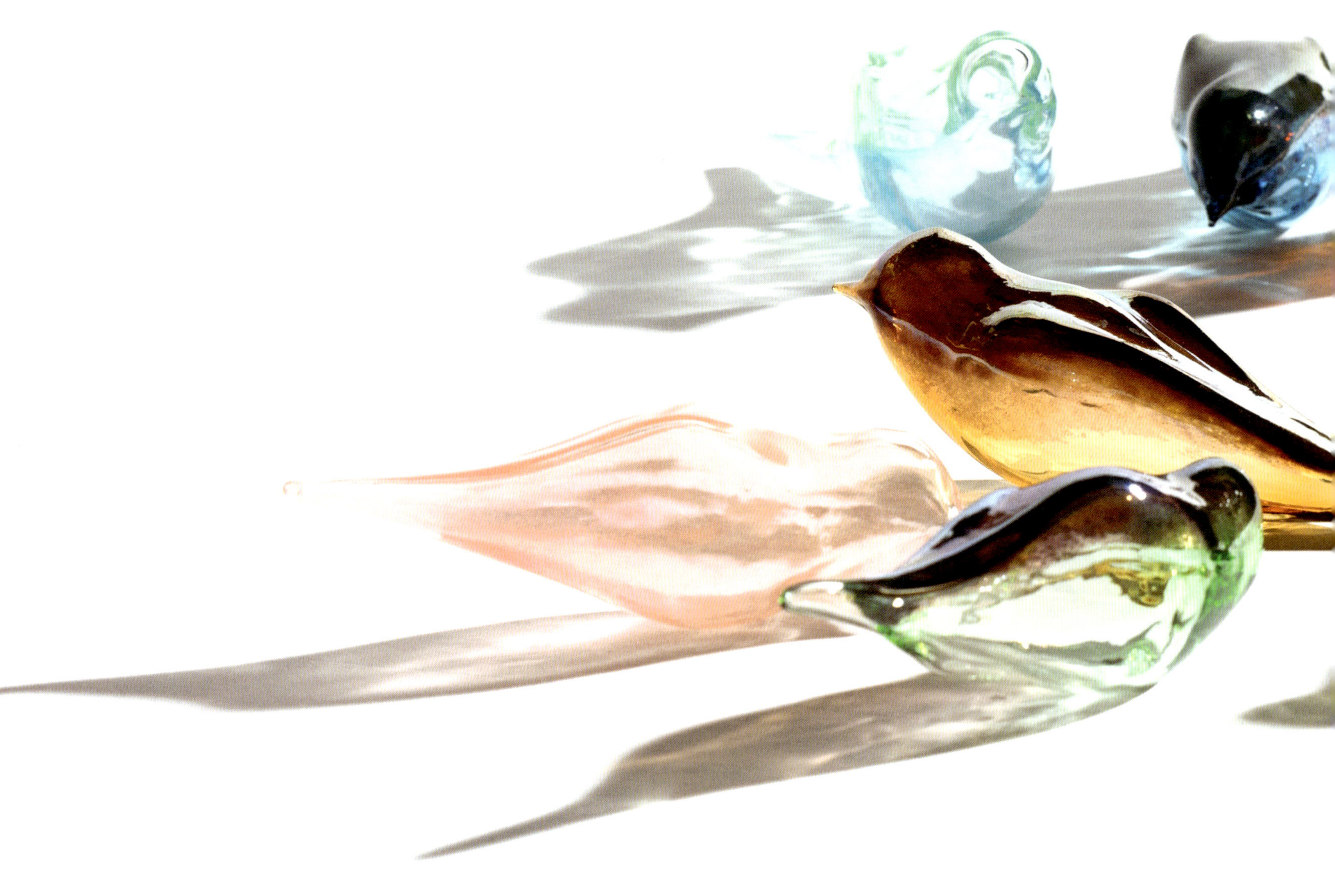

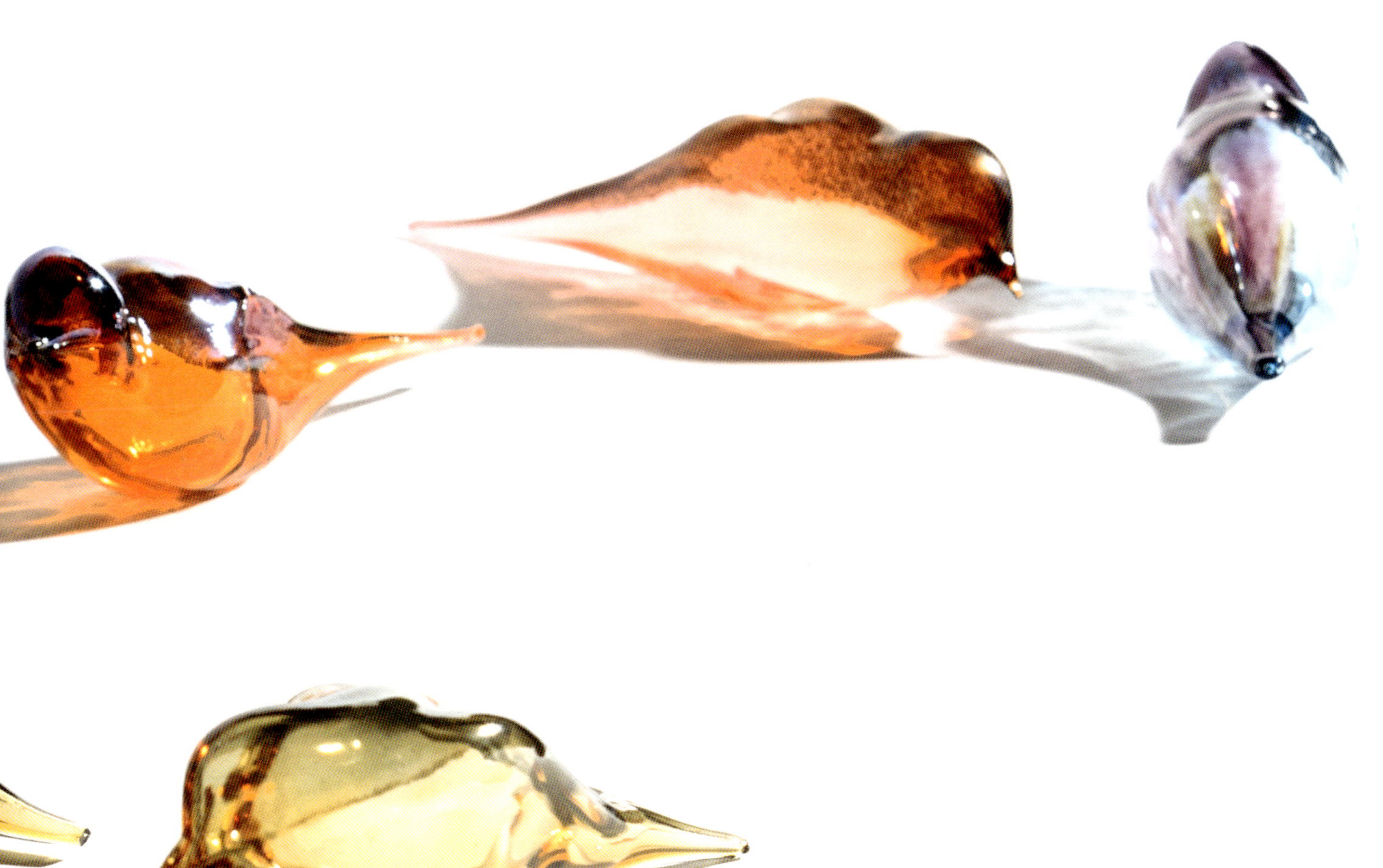

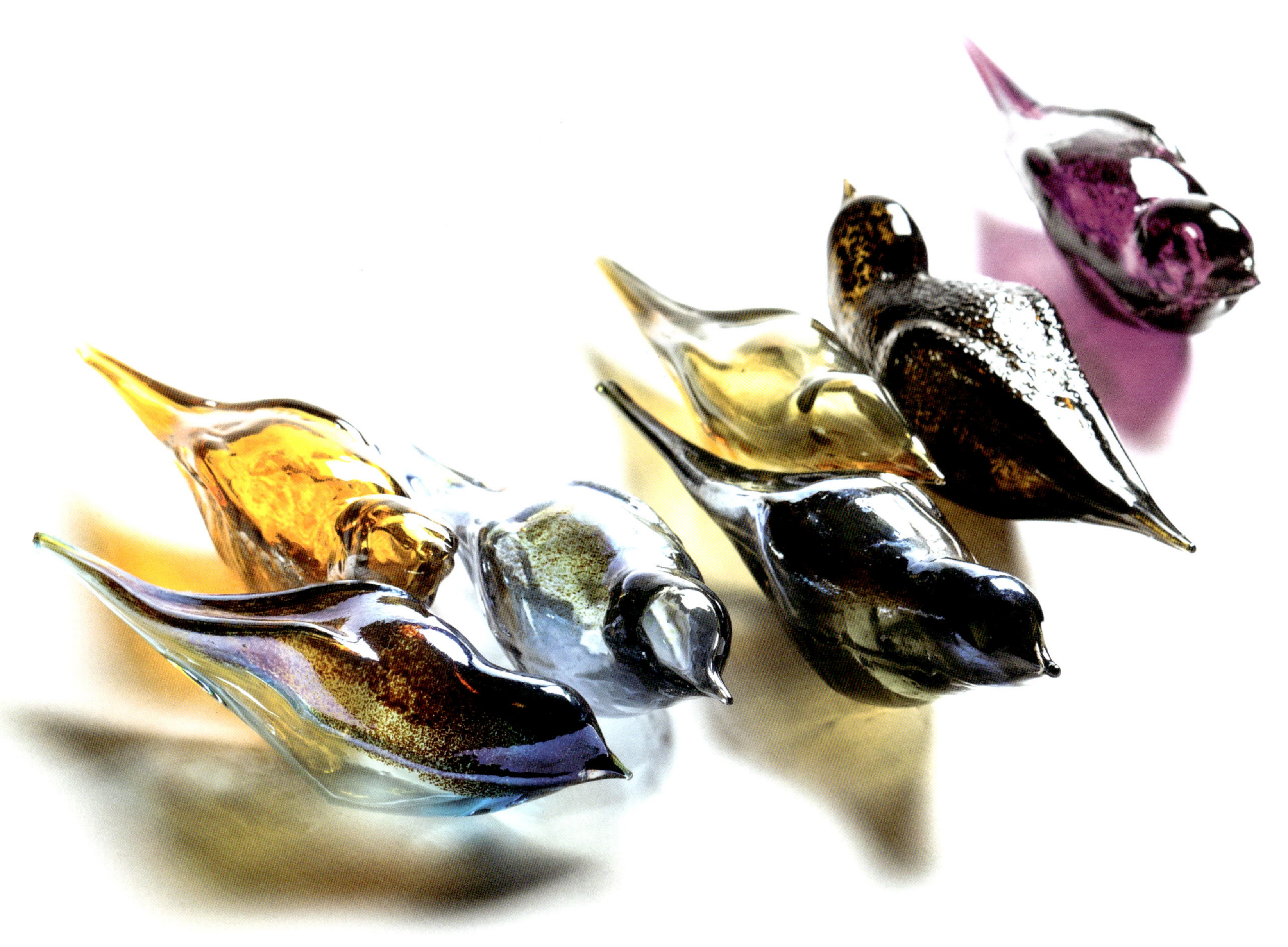

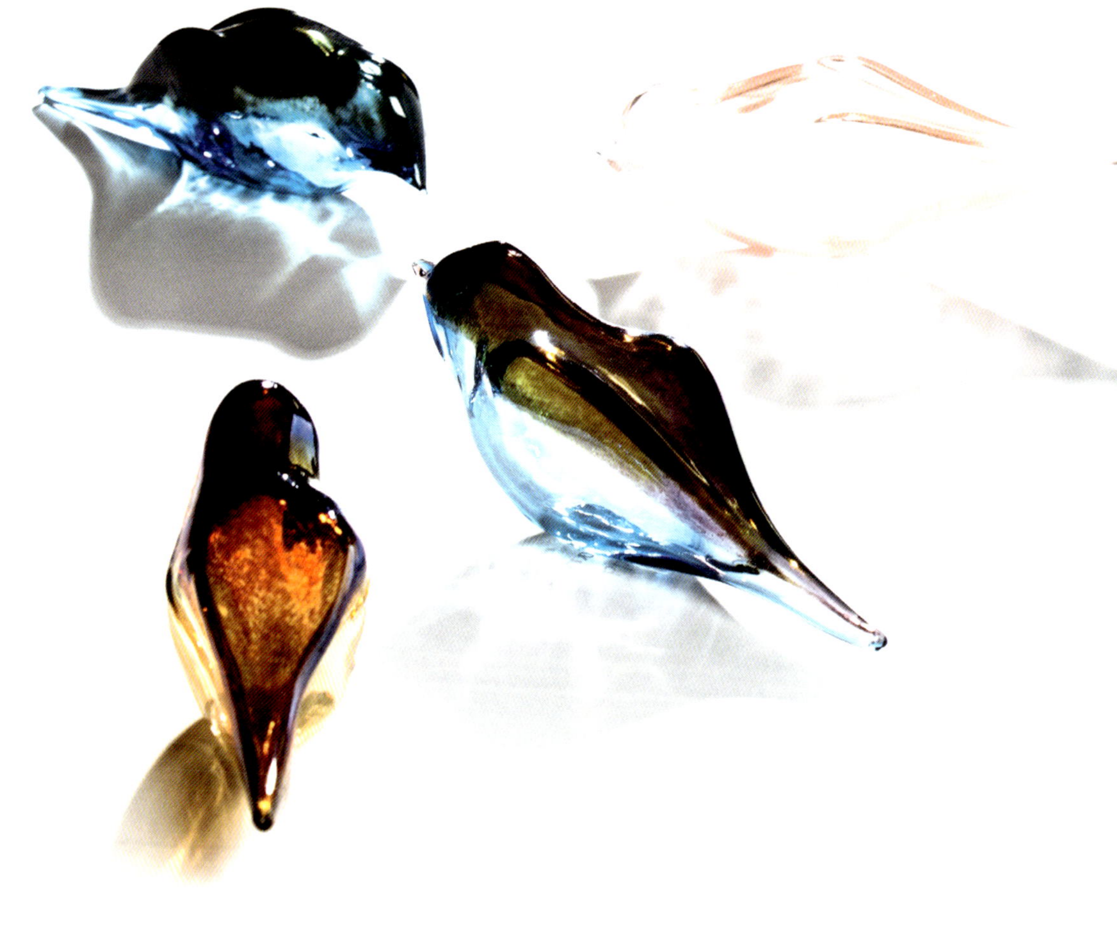

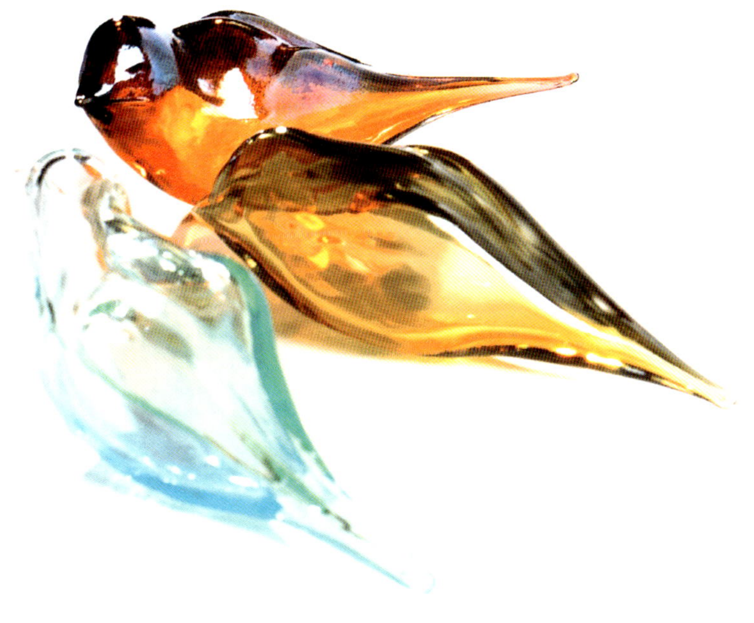

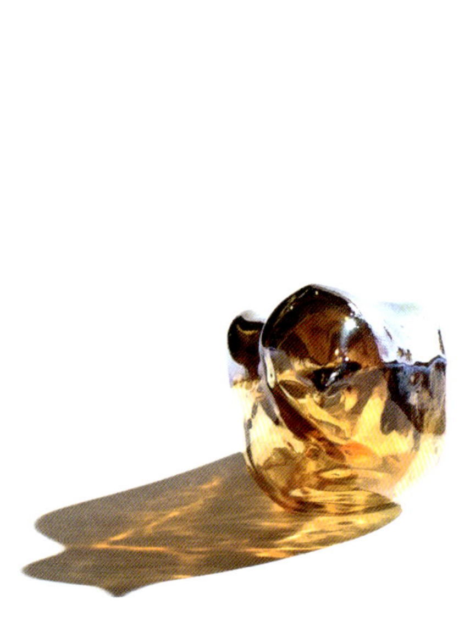
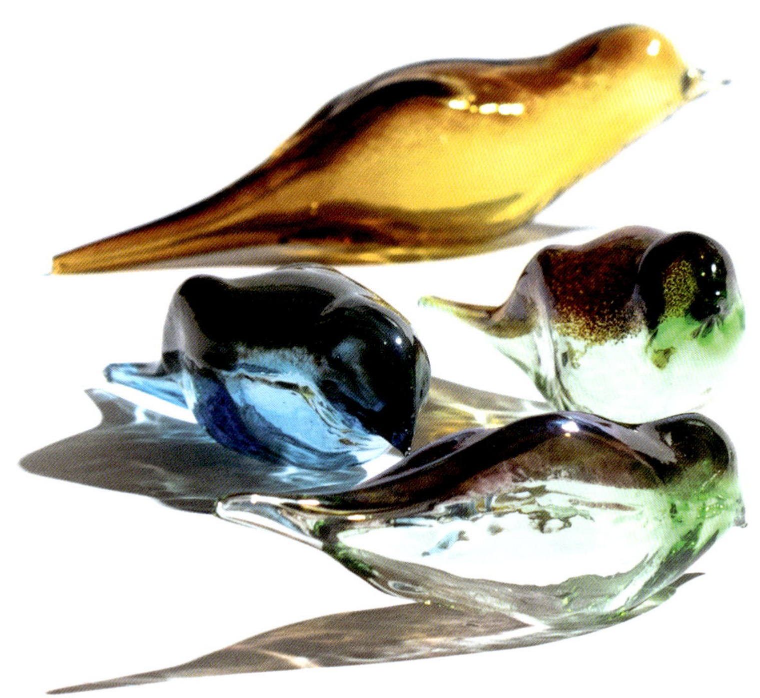

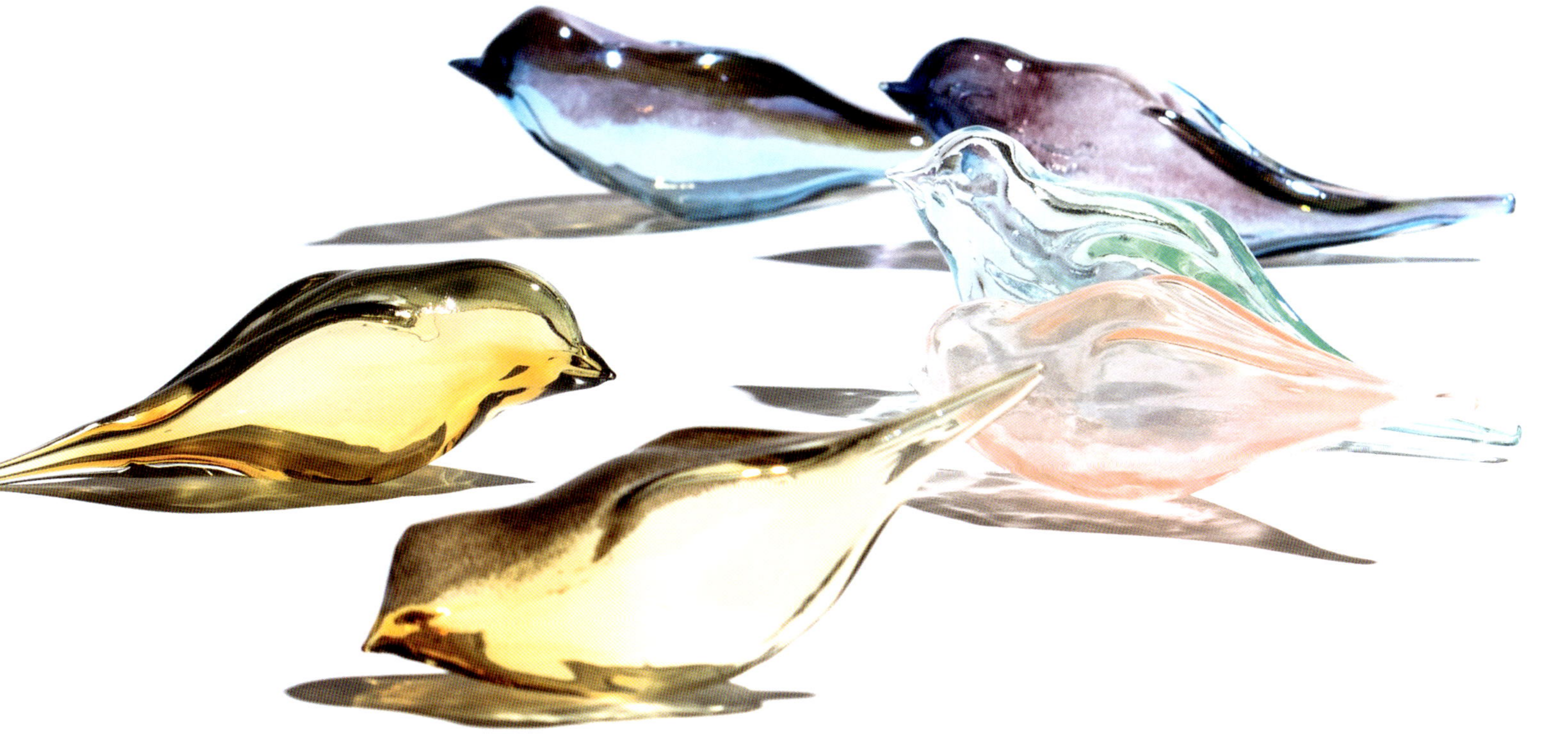

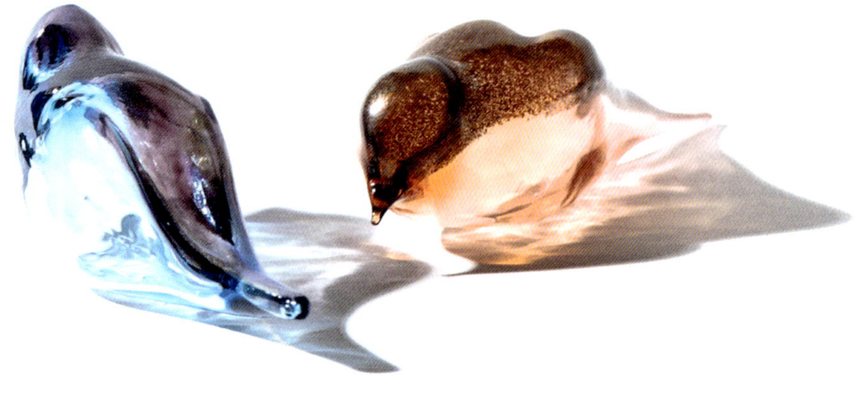

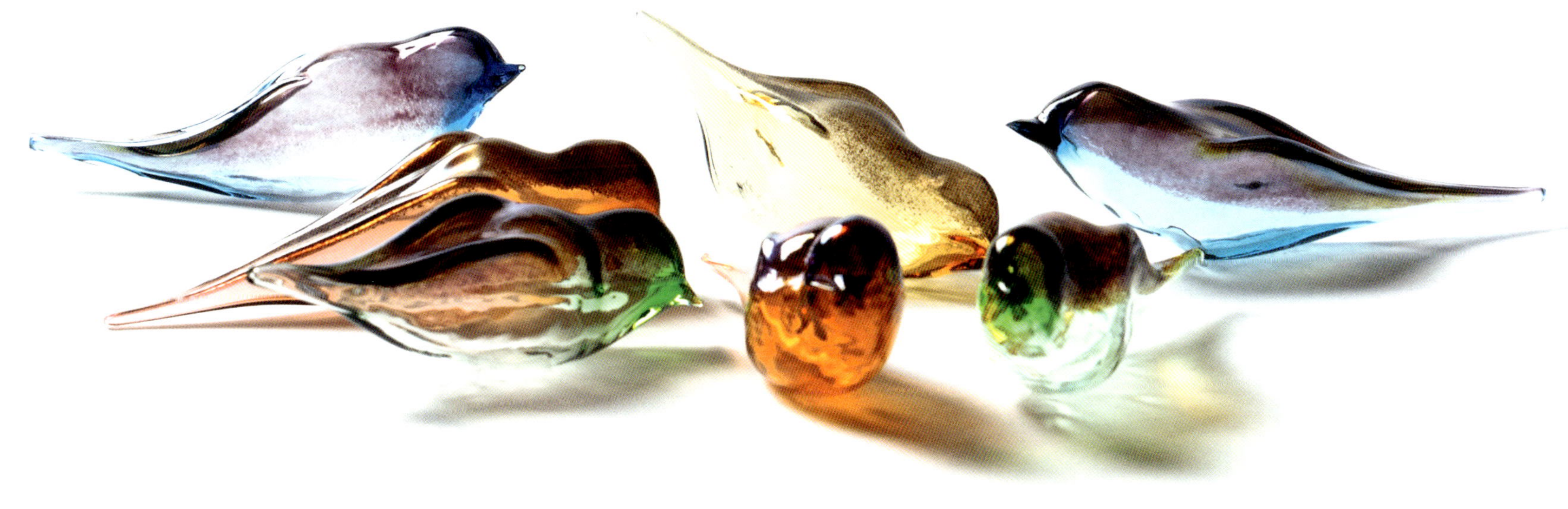

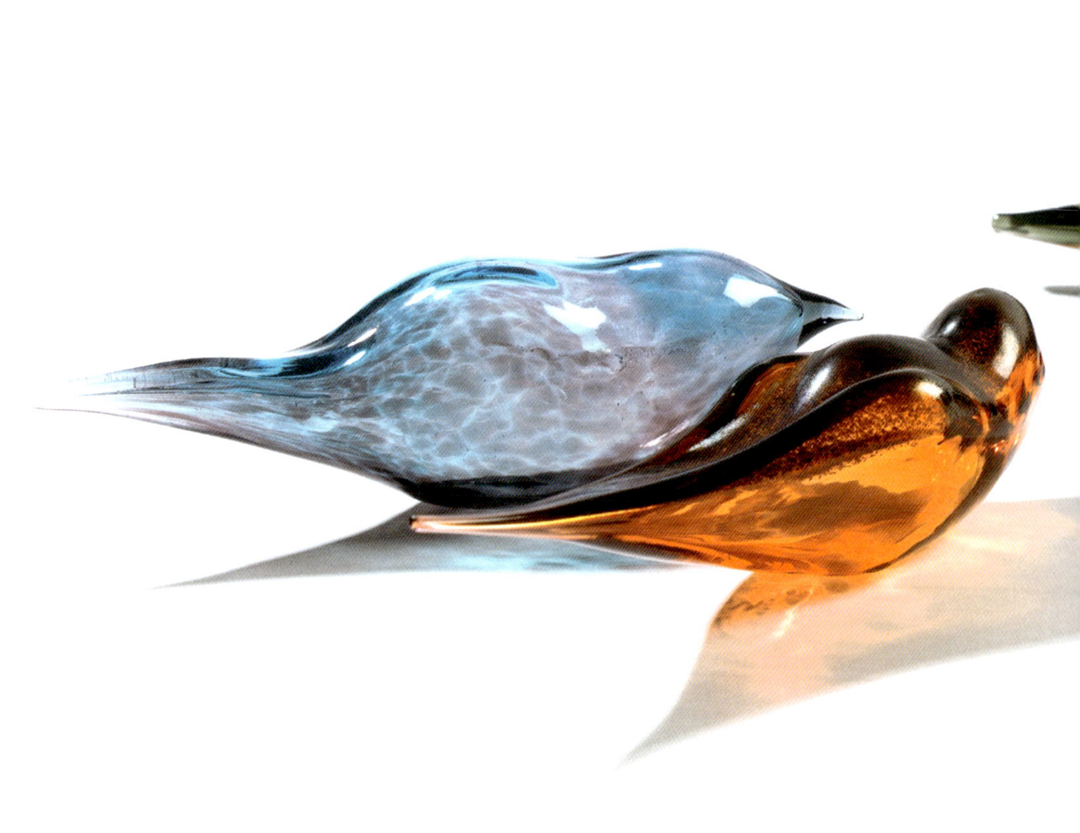

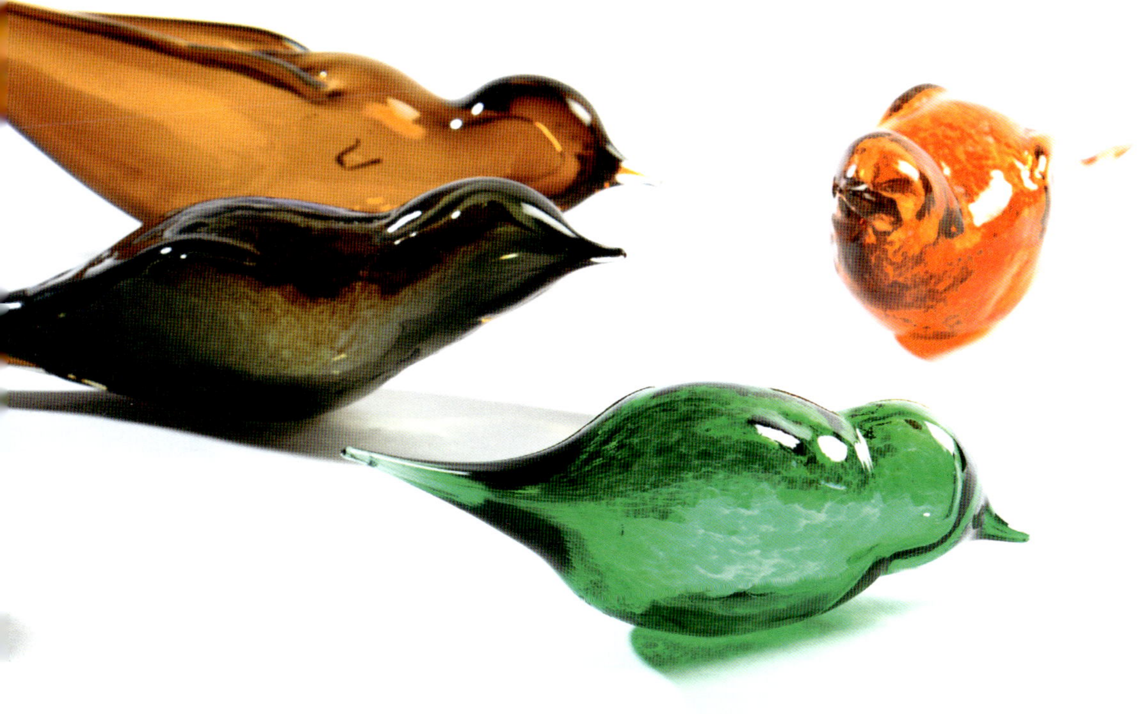

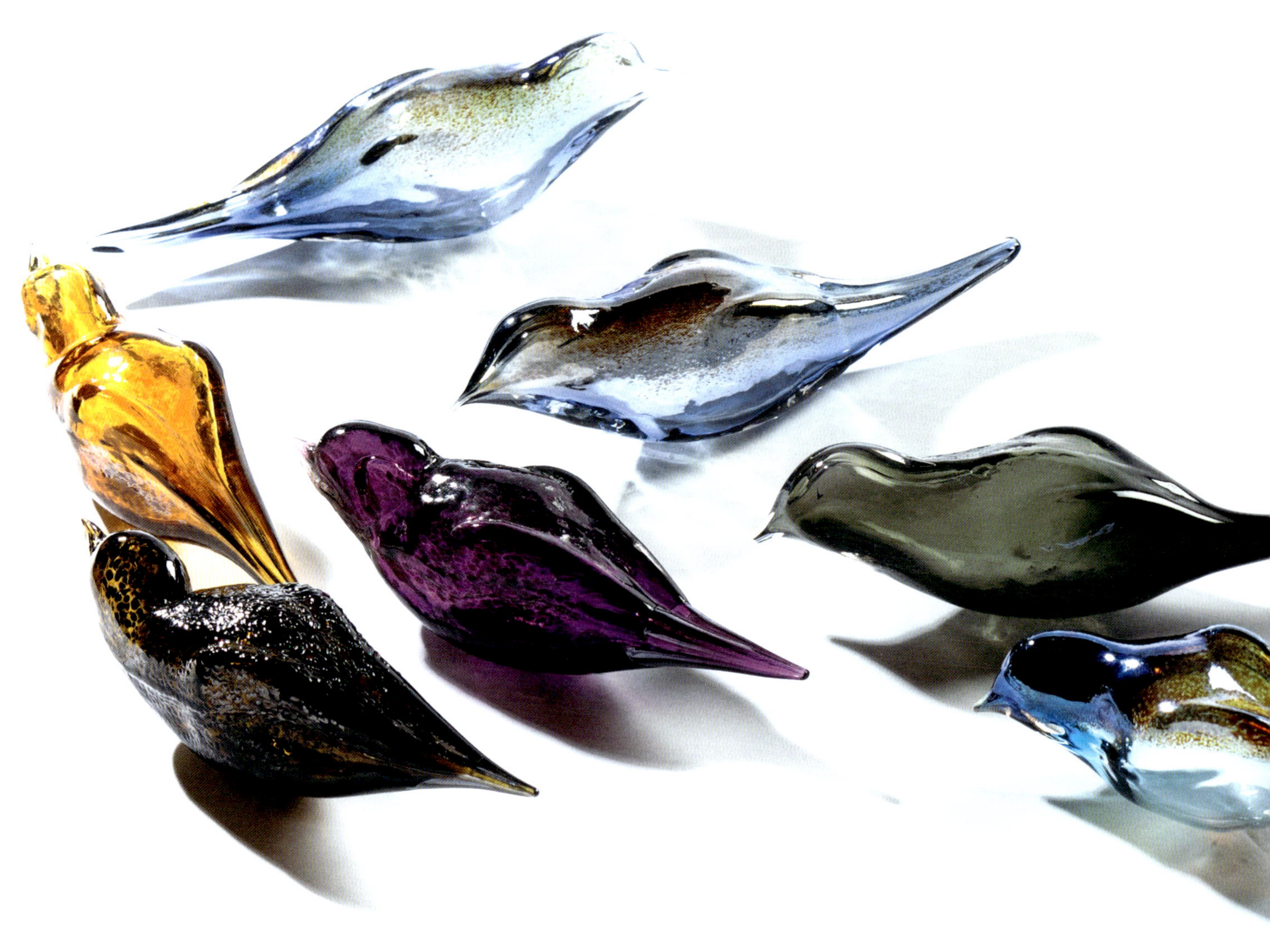

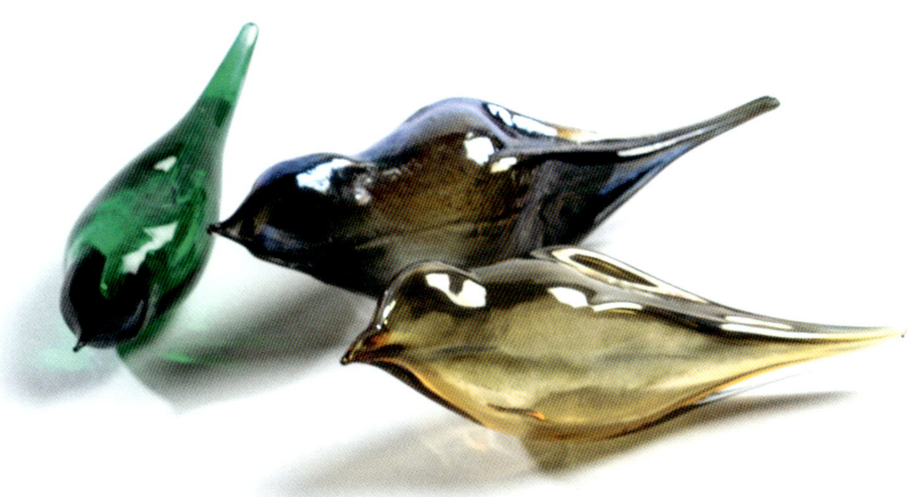

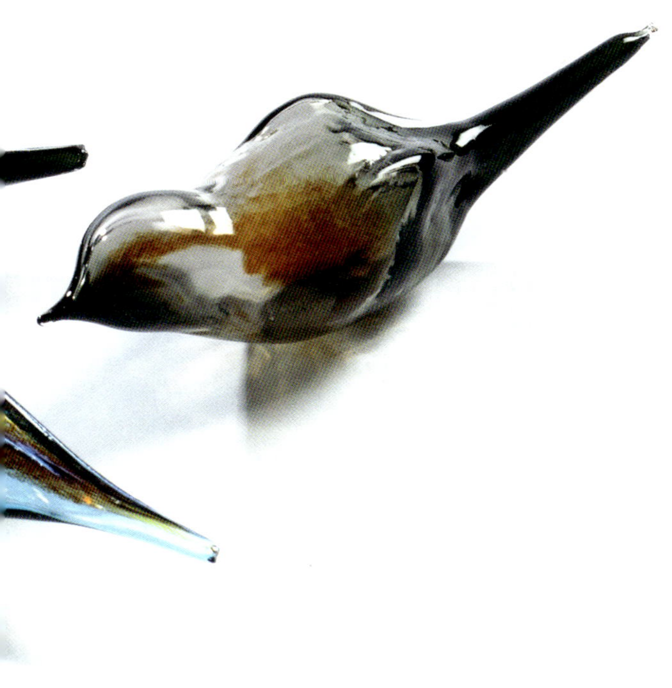

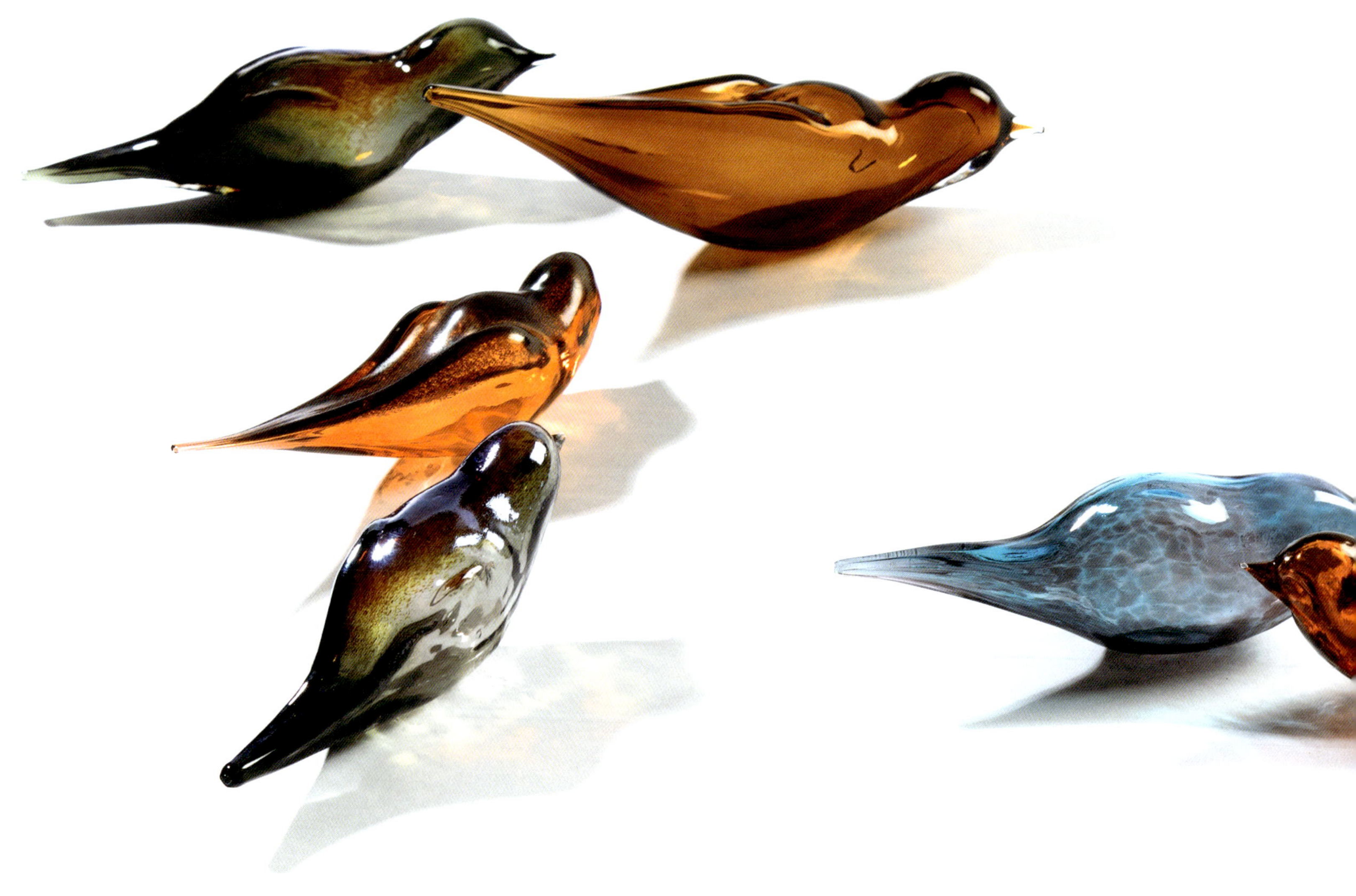

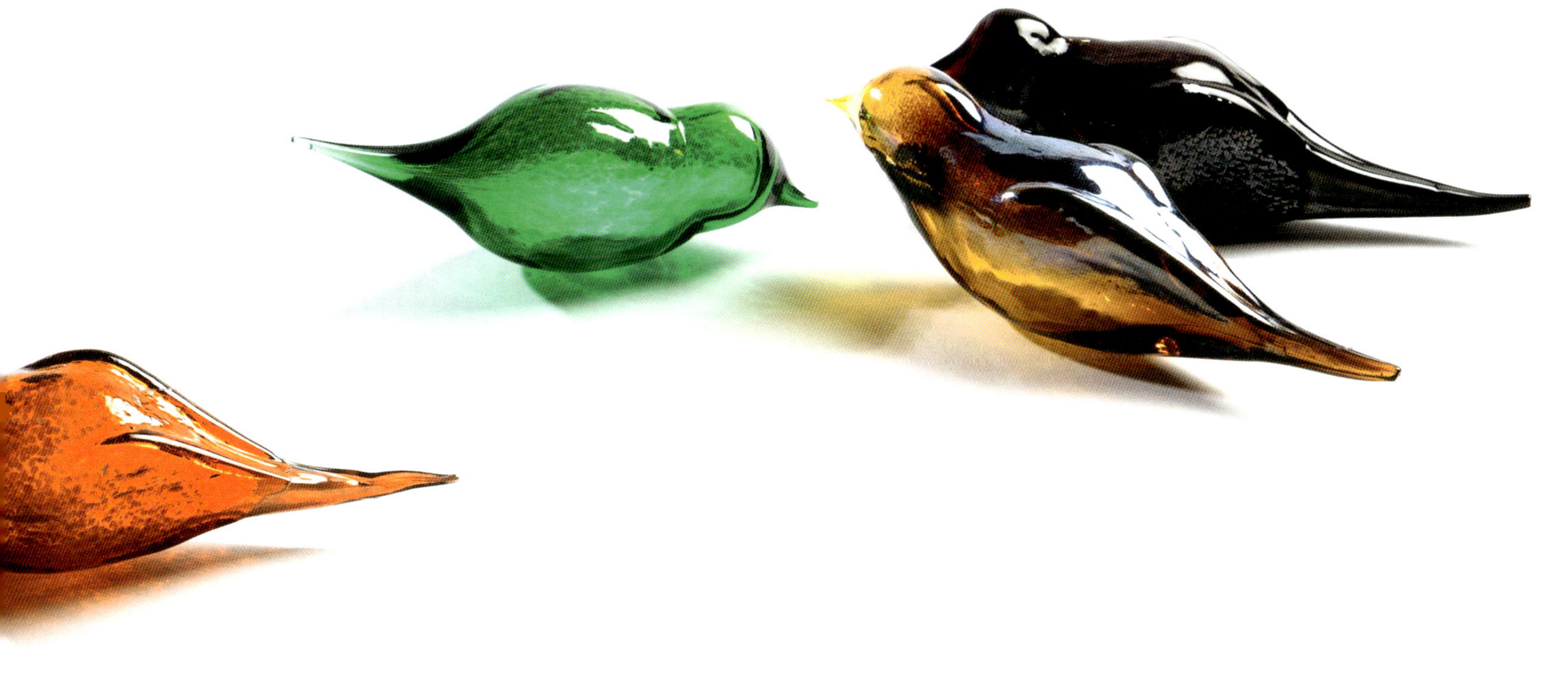

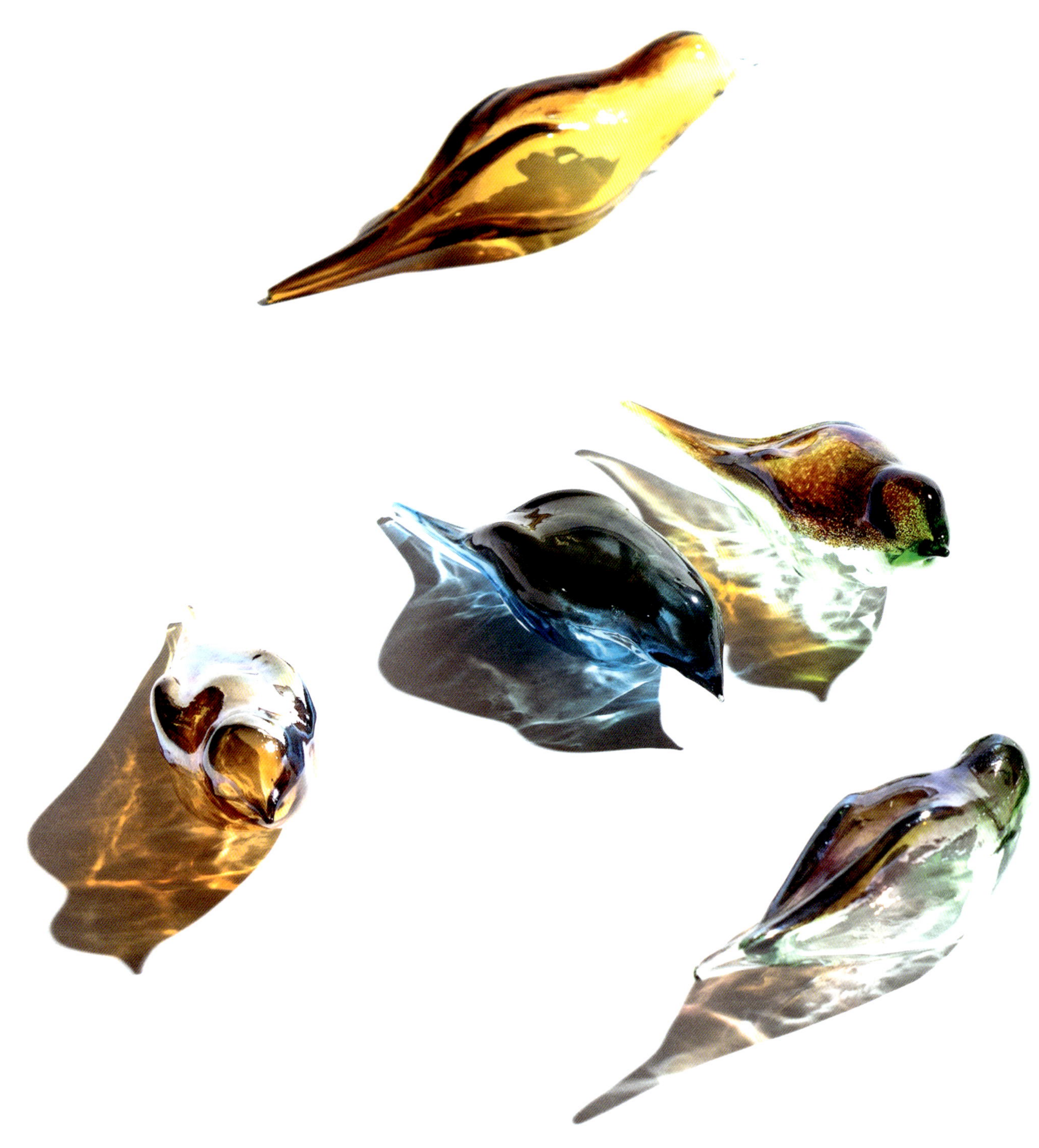

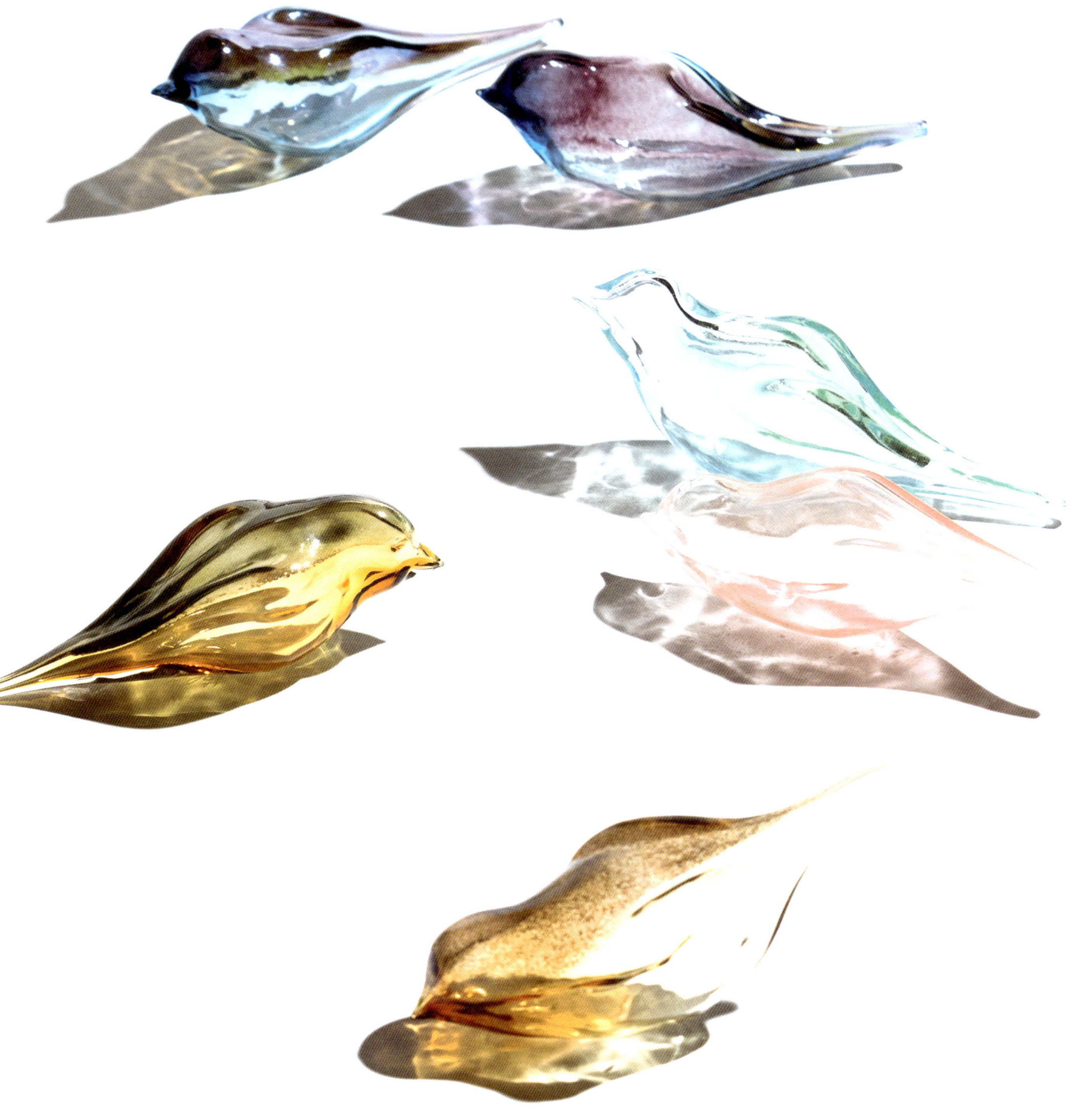

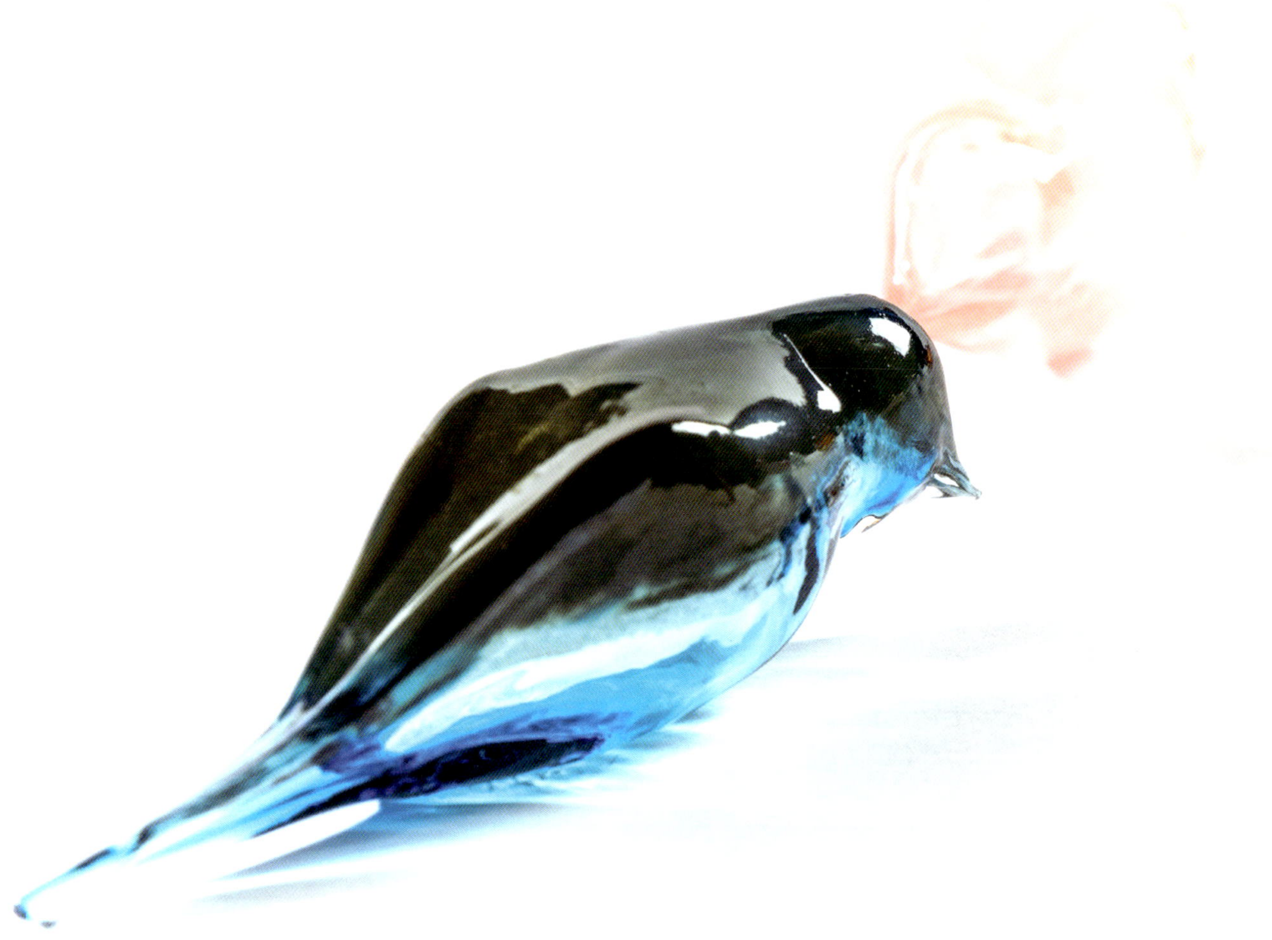

beloved

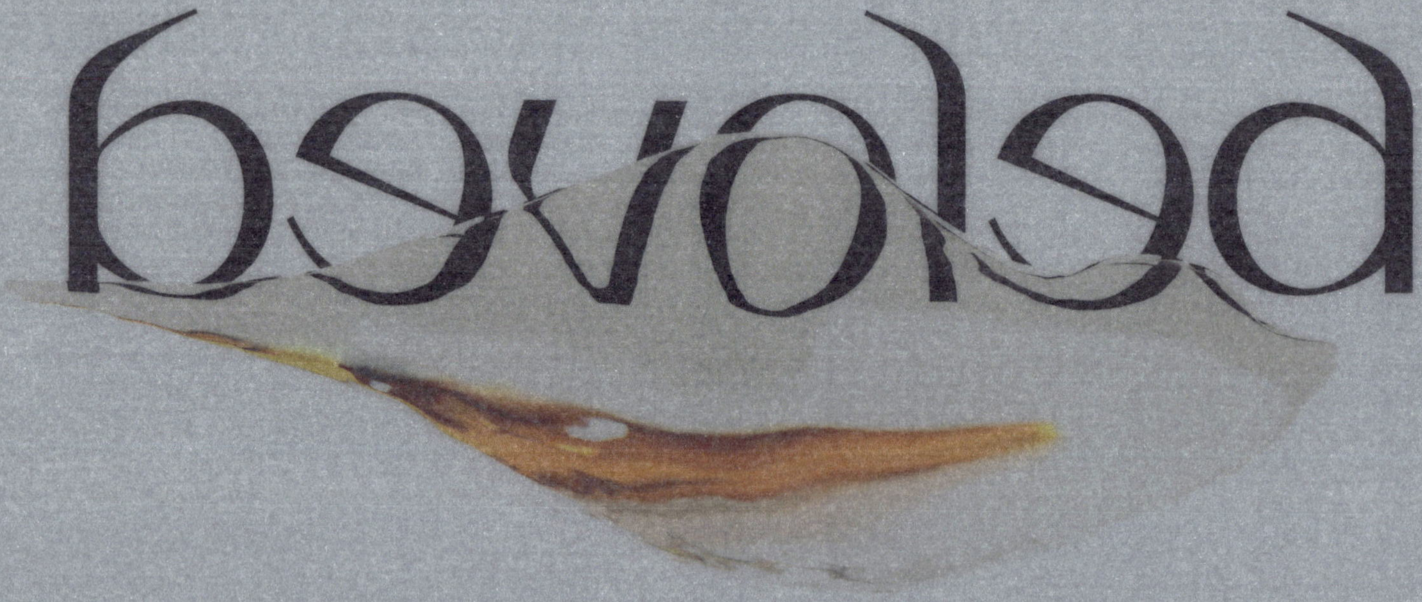

beloved

70

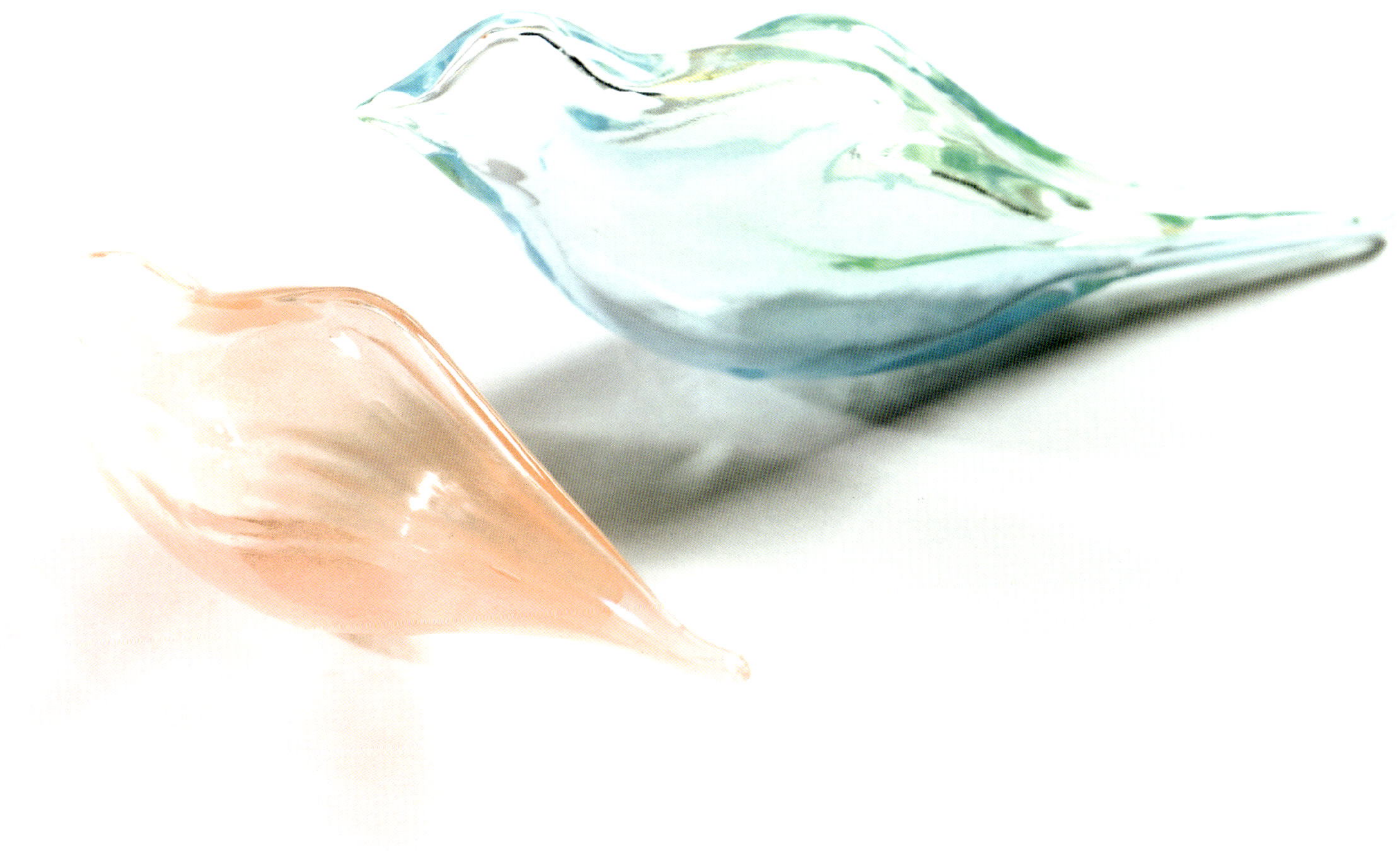

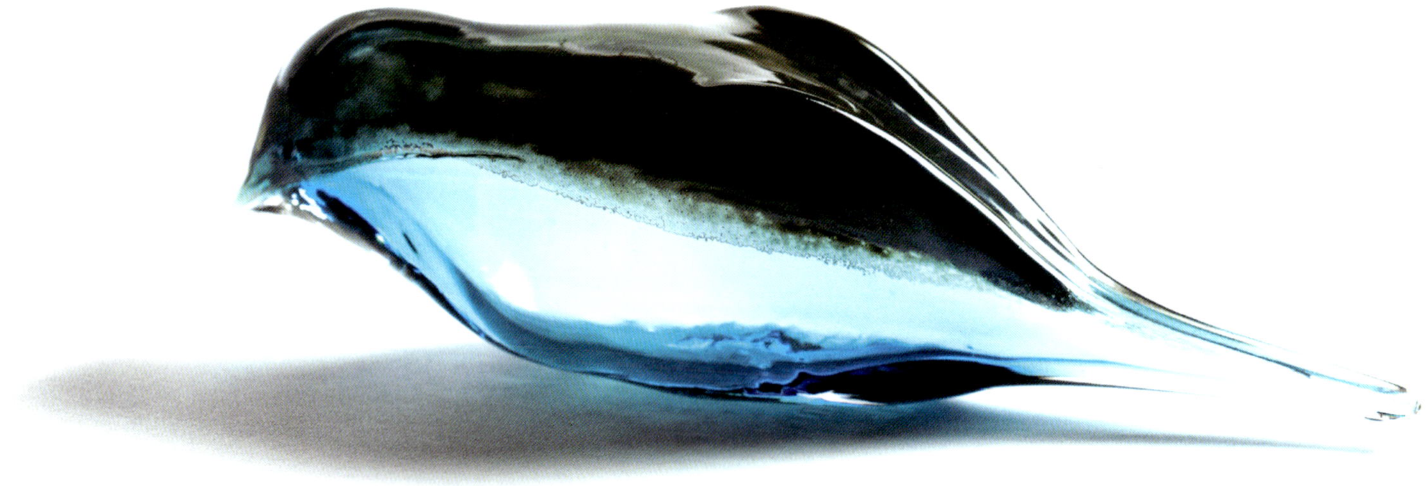

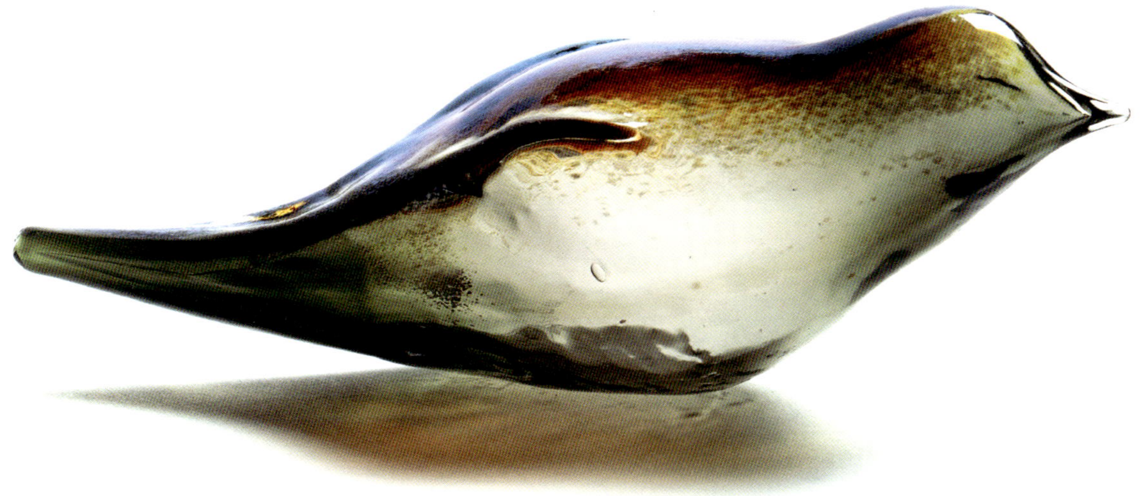

74

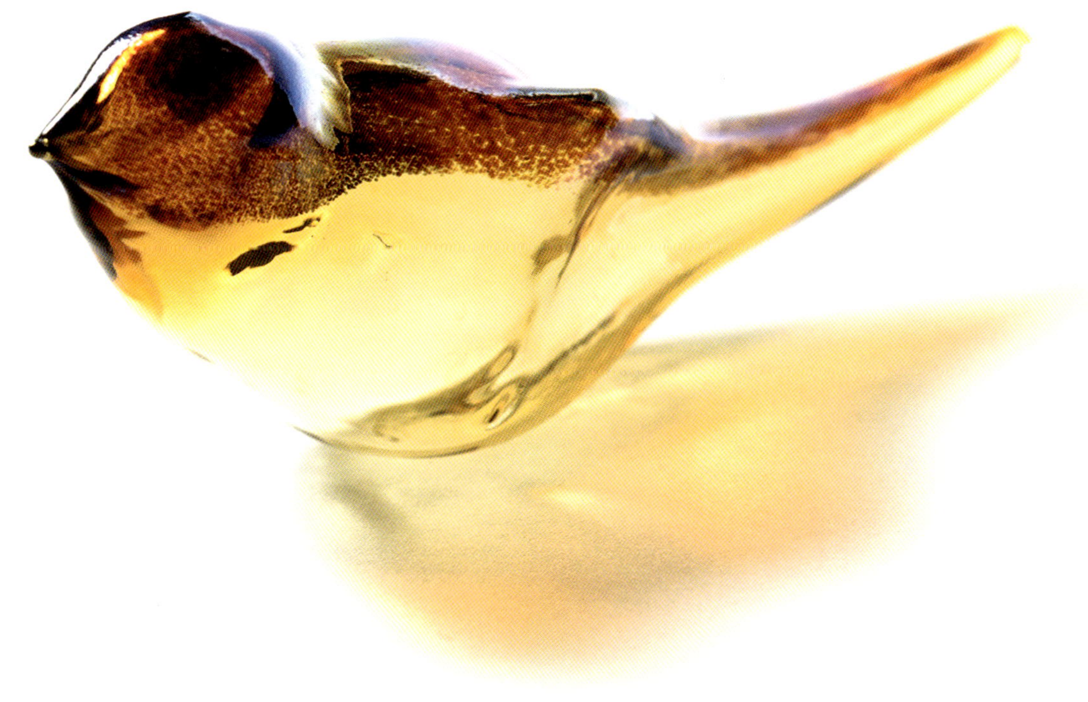

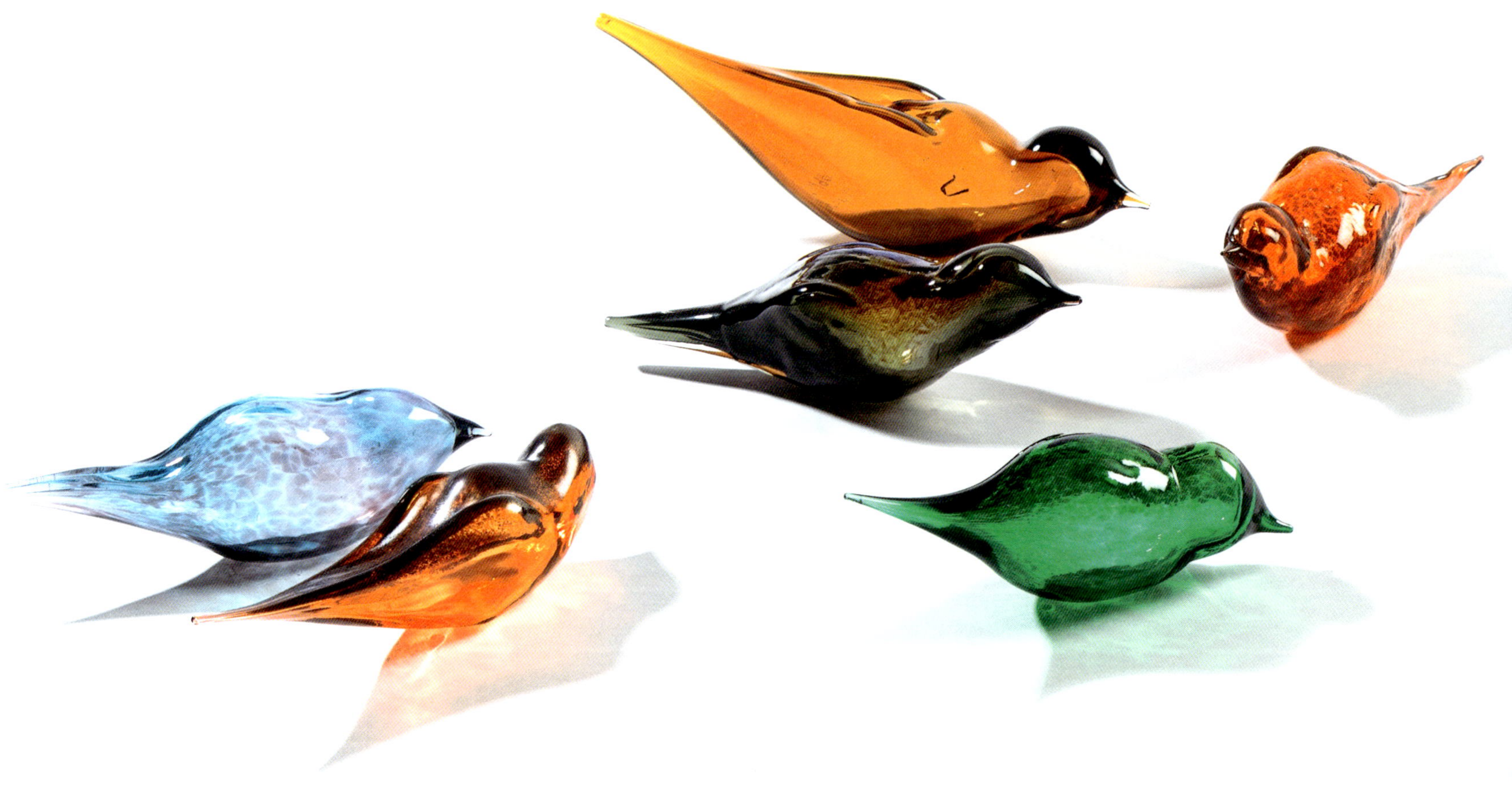

removed

removed

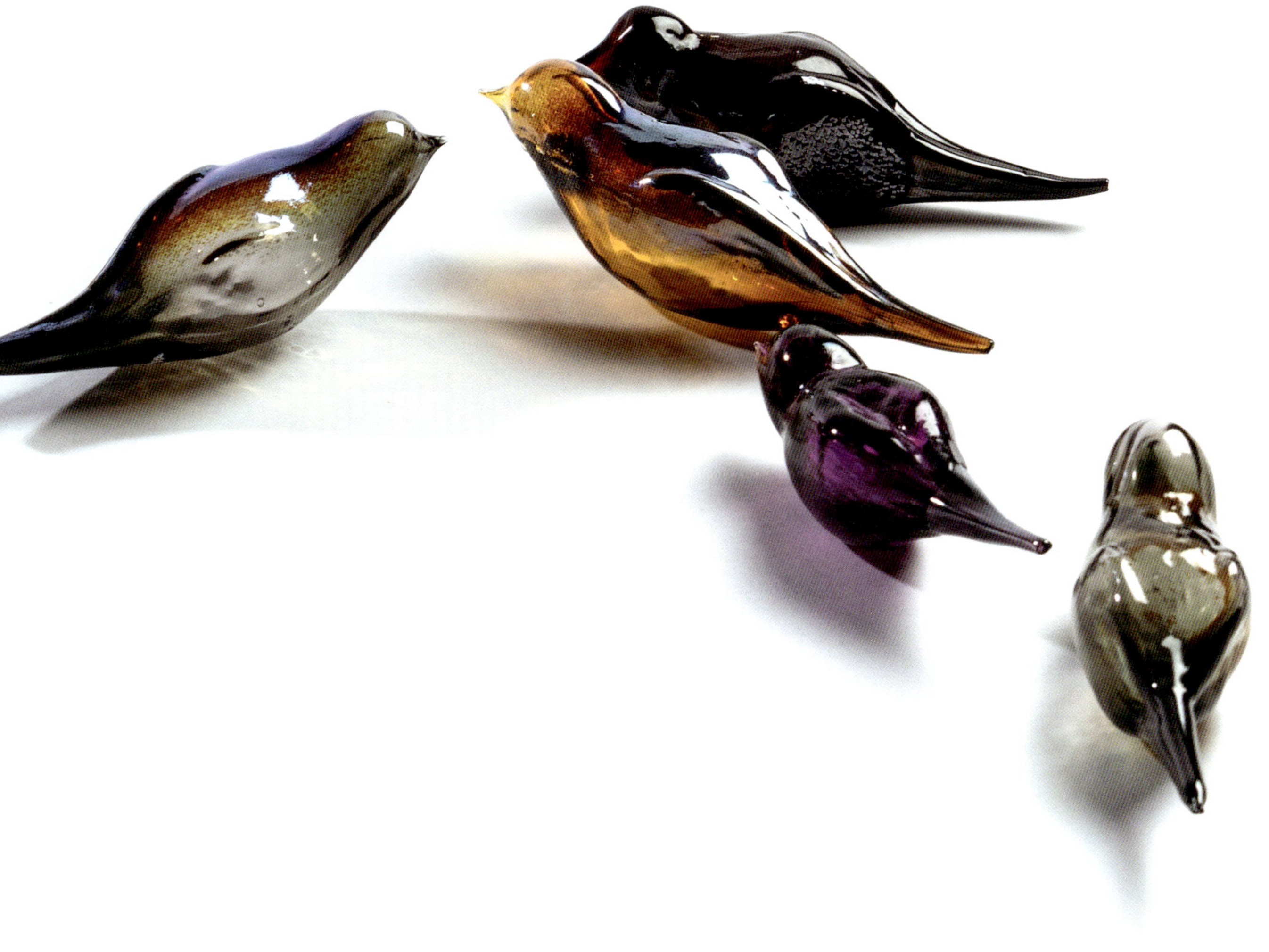

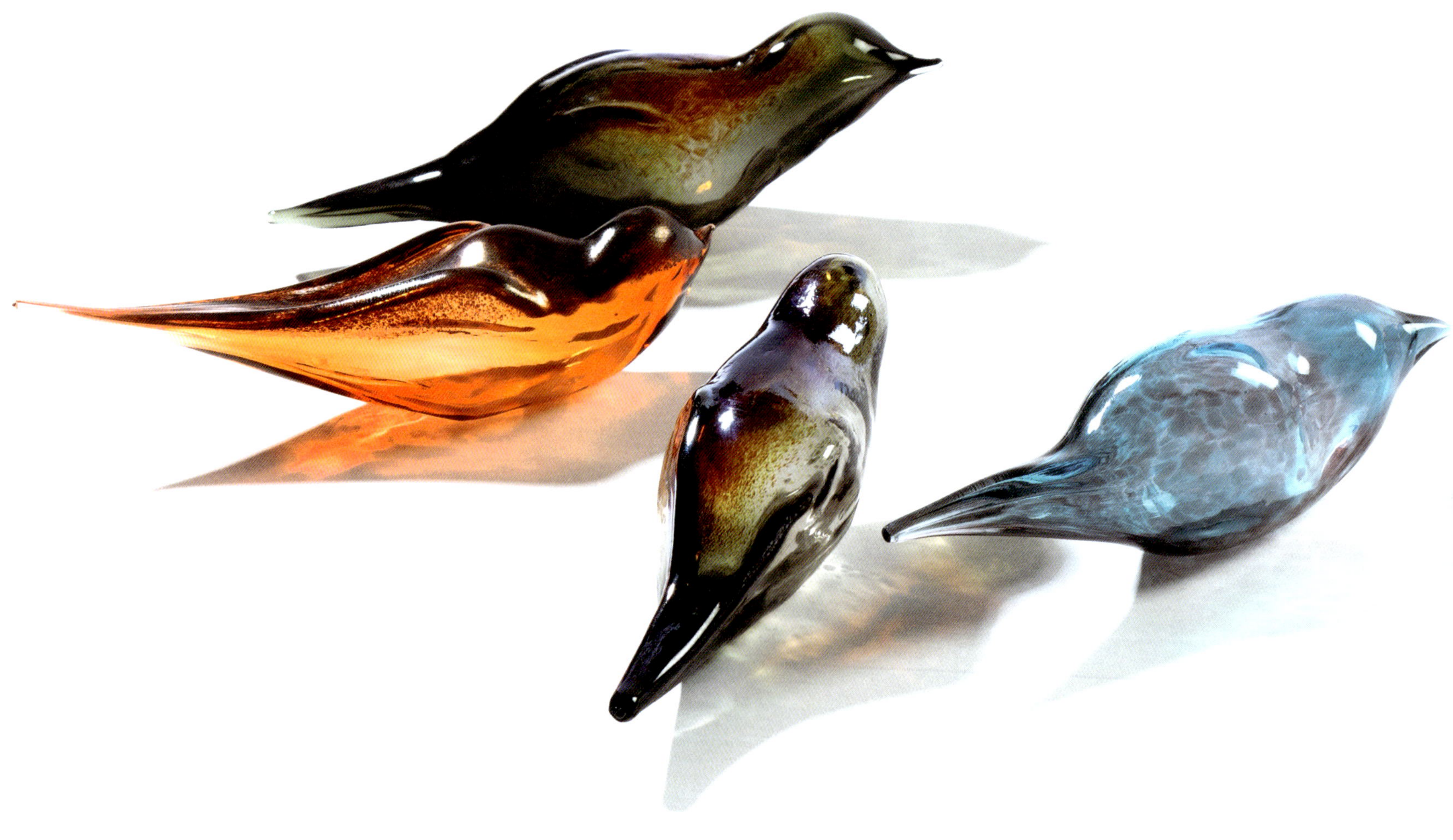

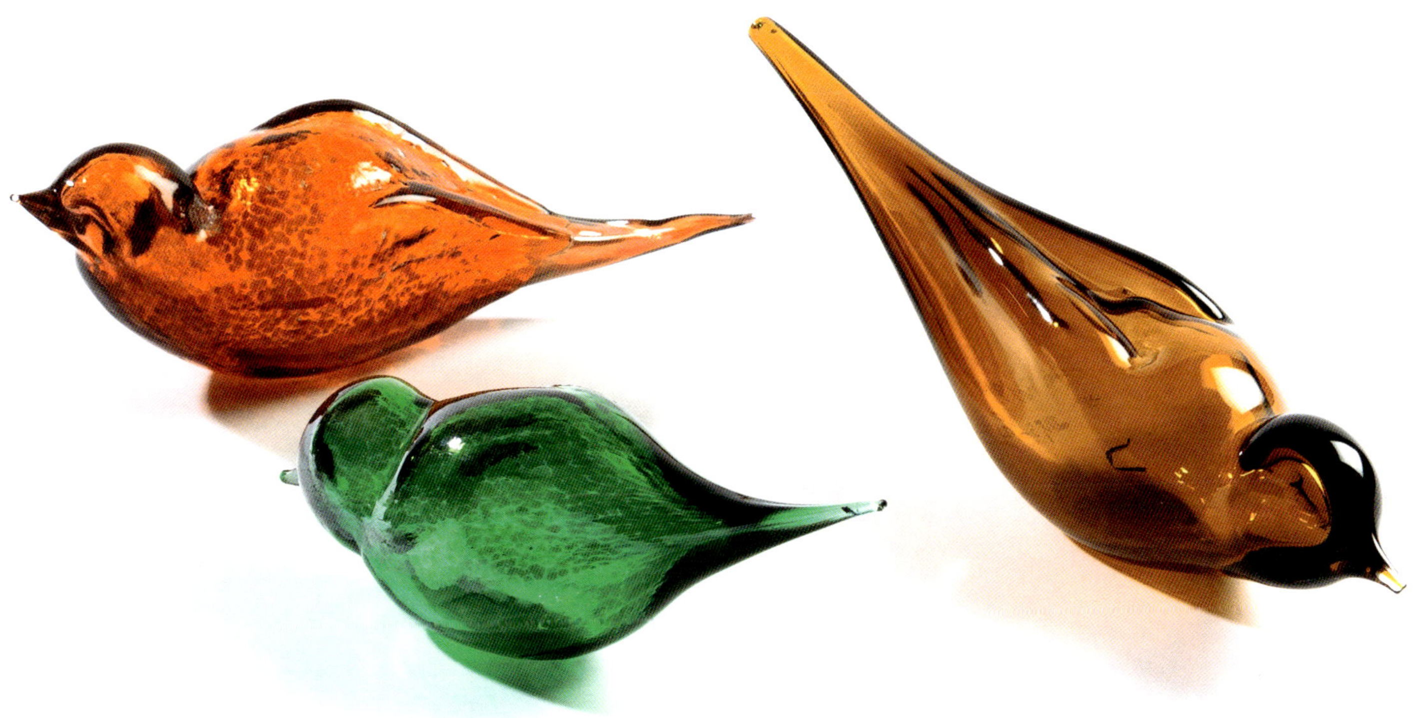

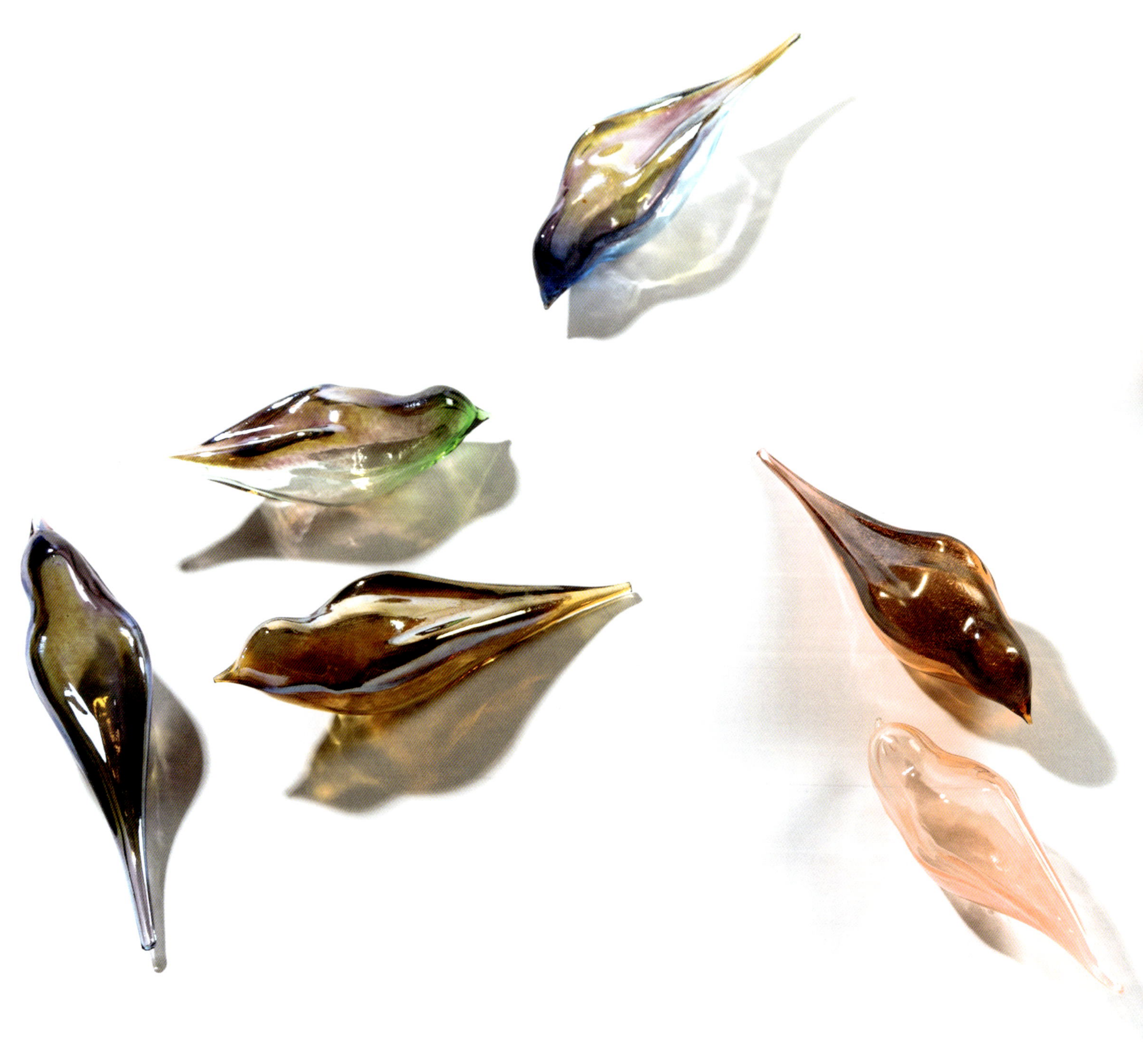

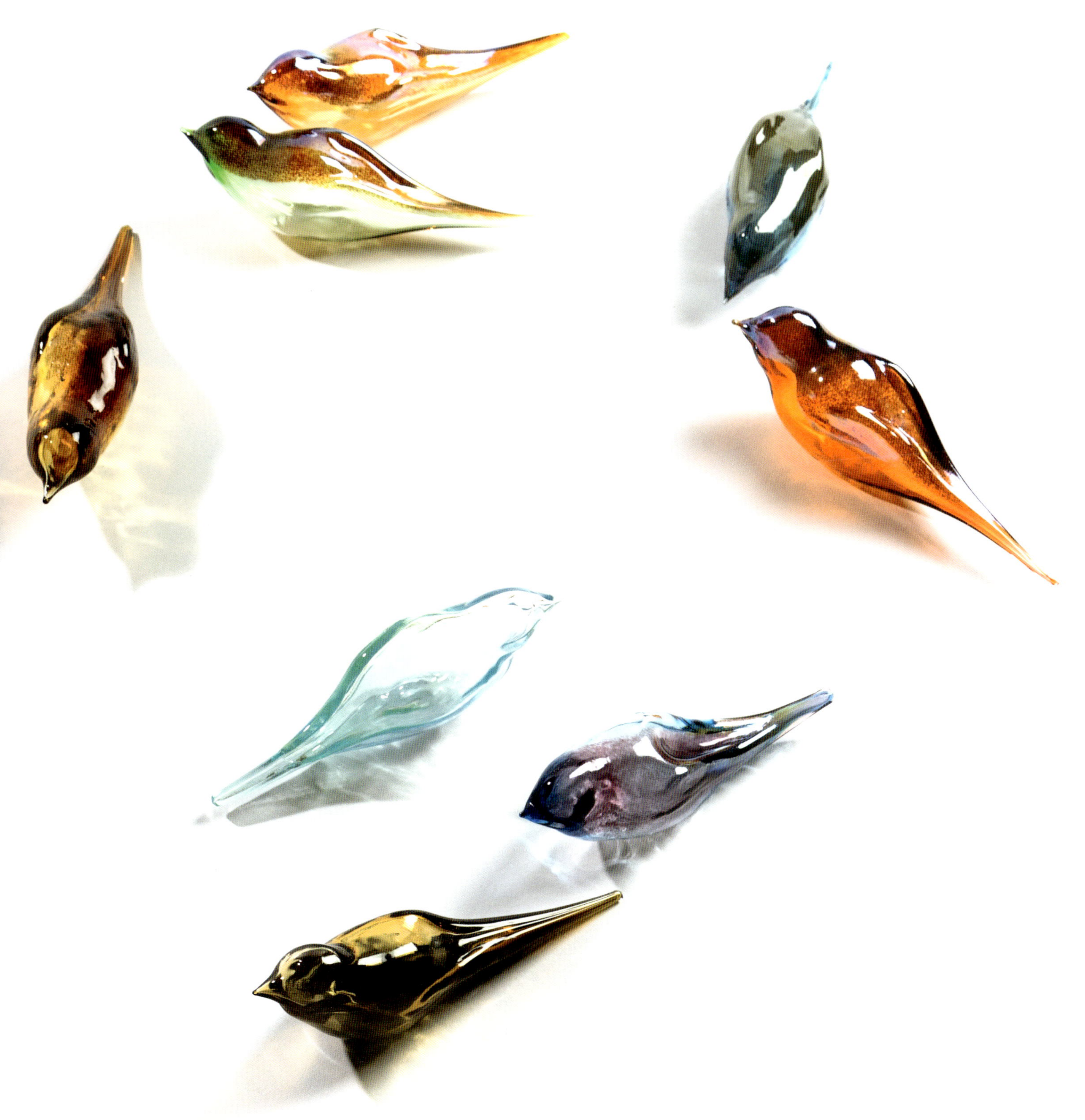

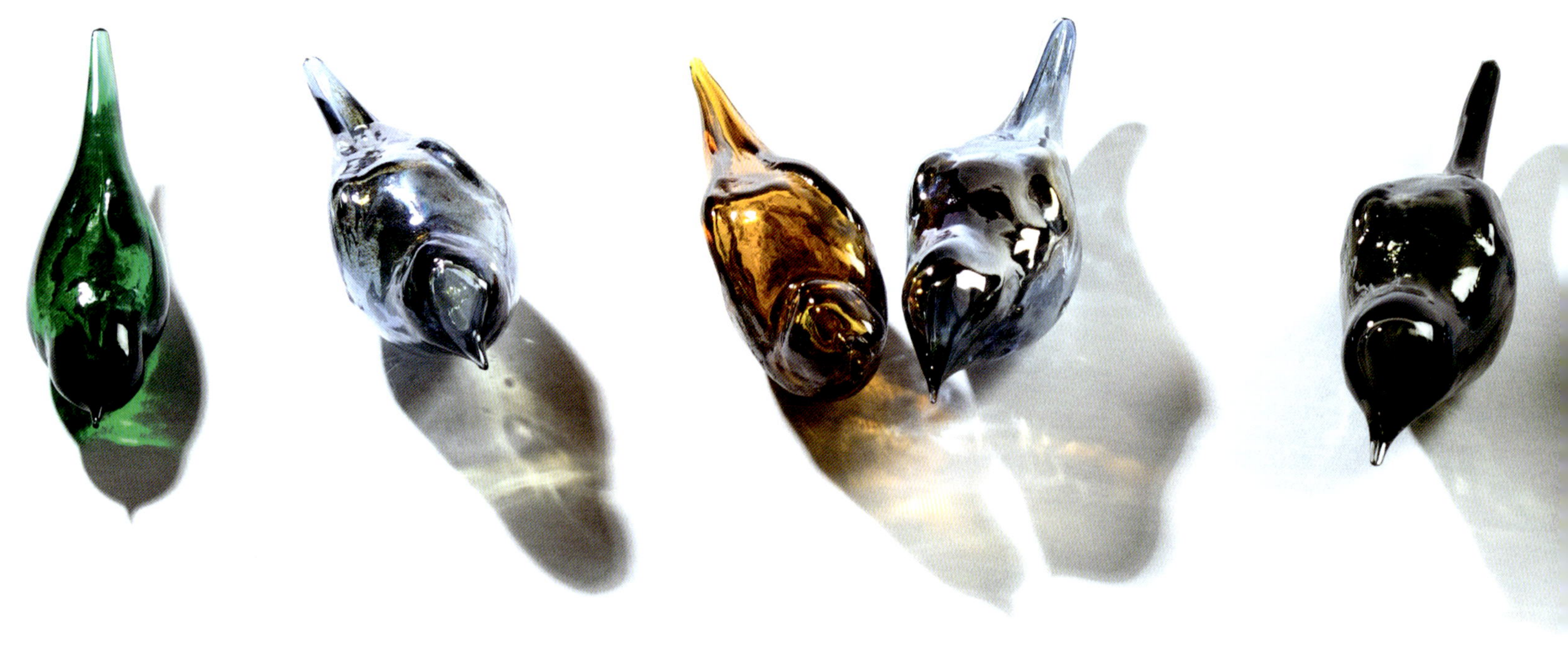

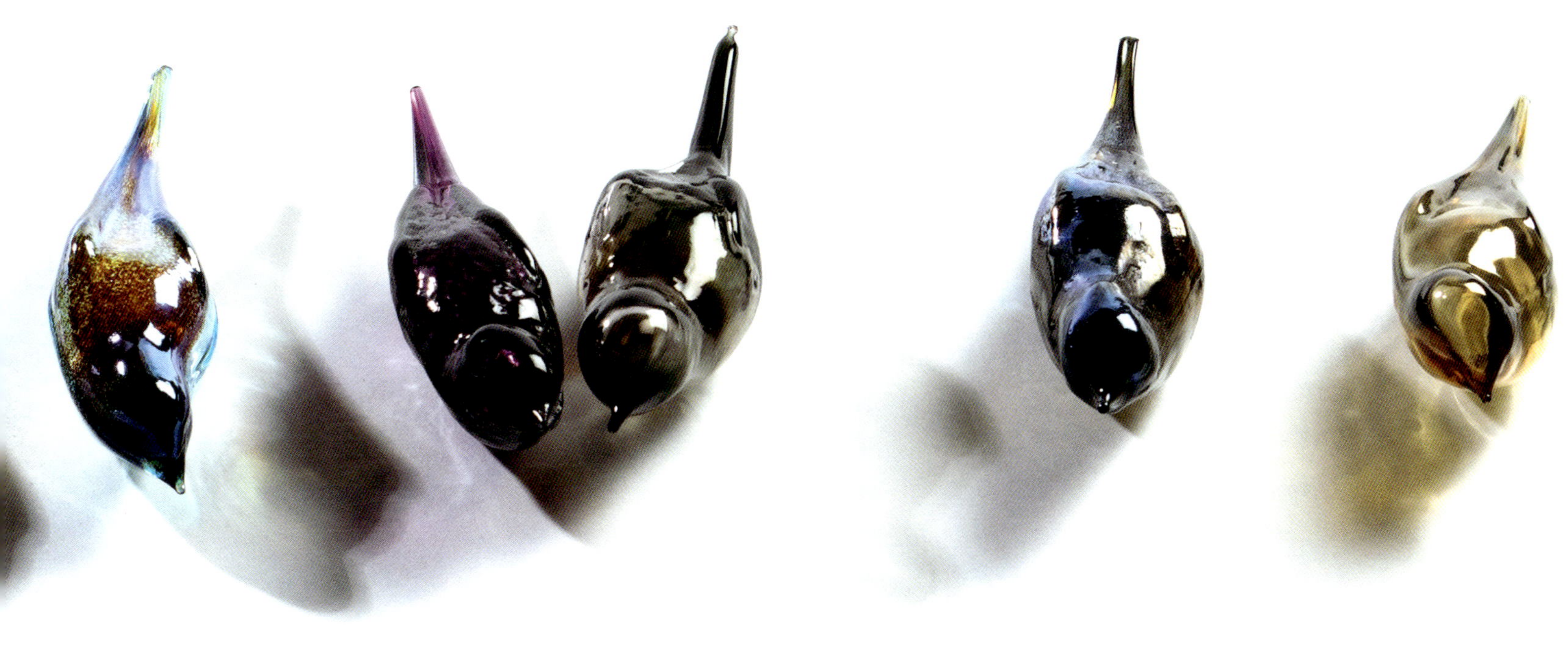

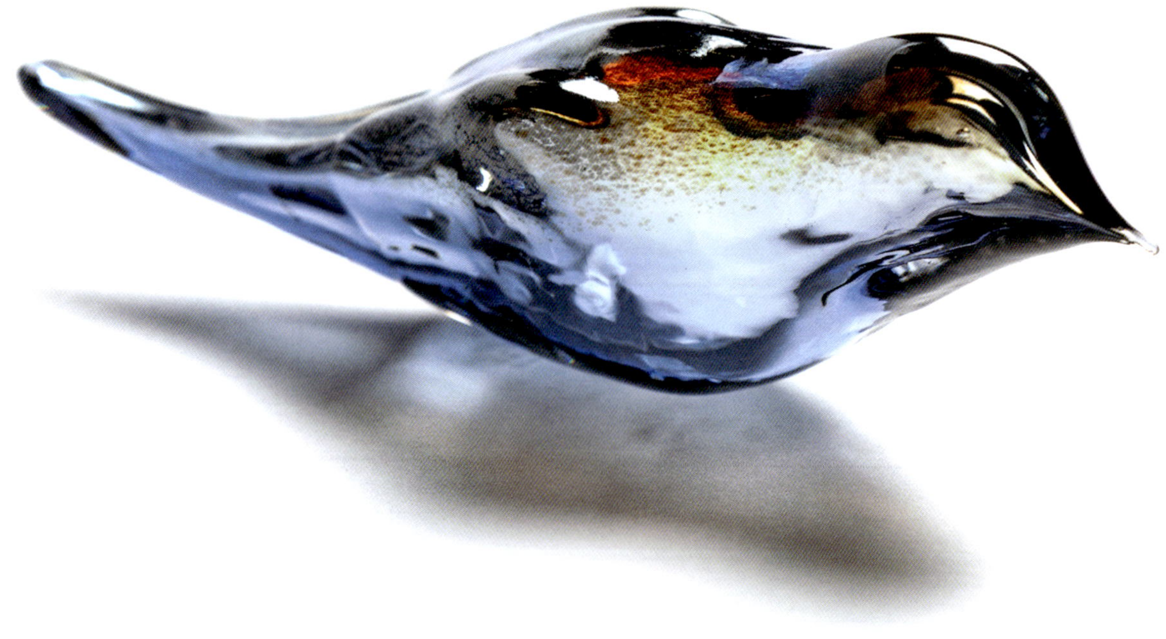

87

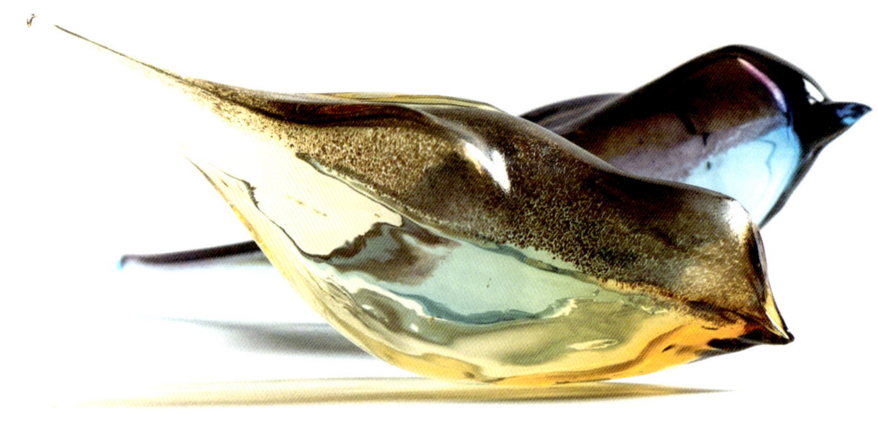

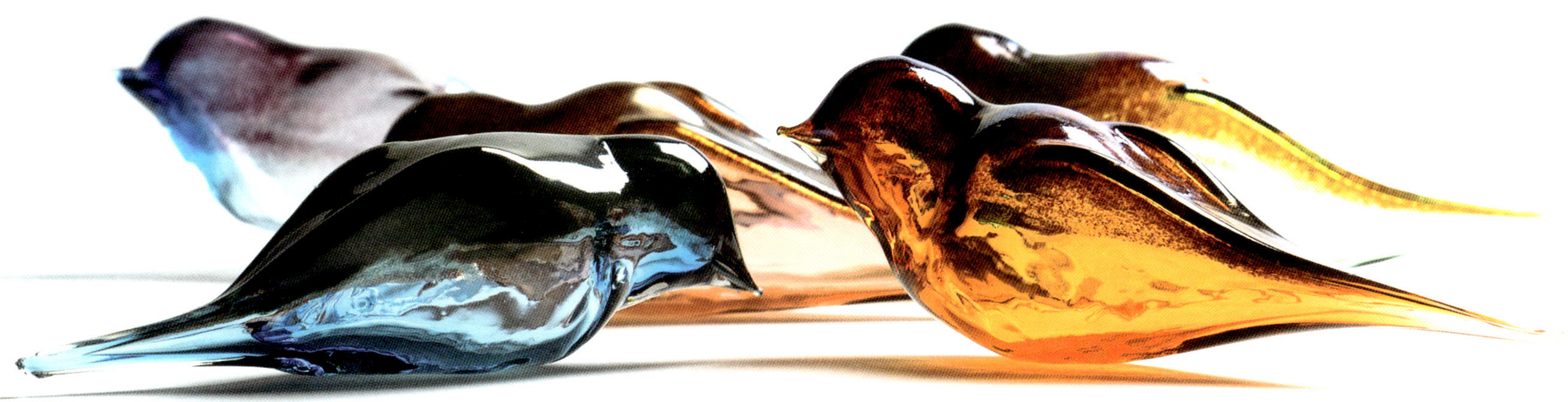

90

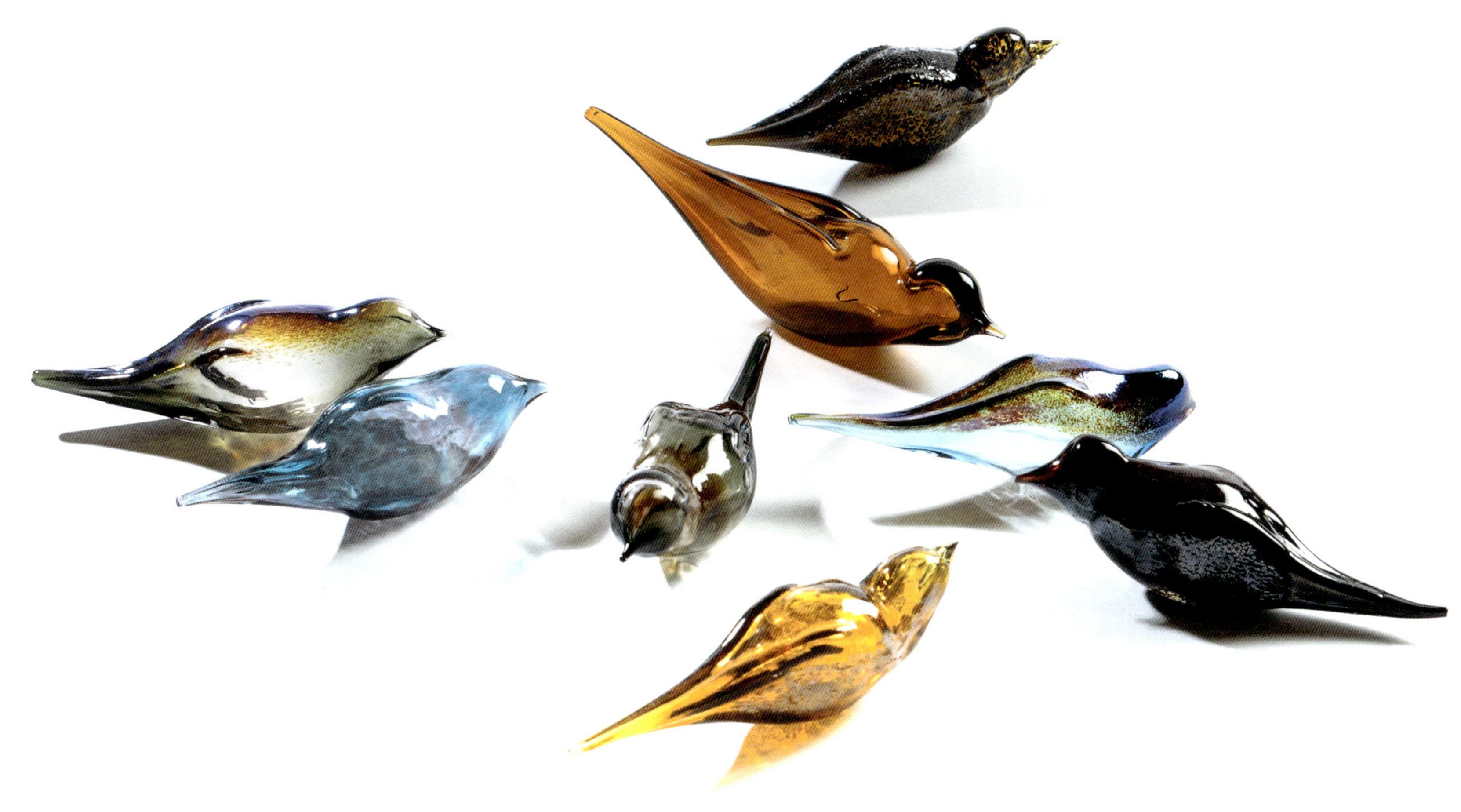

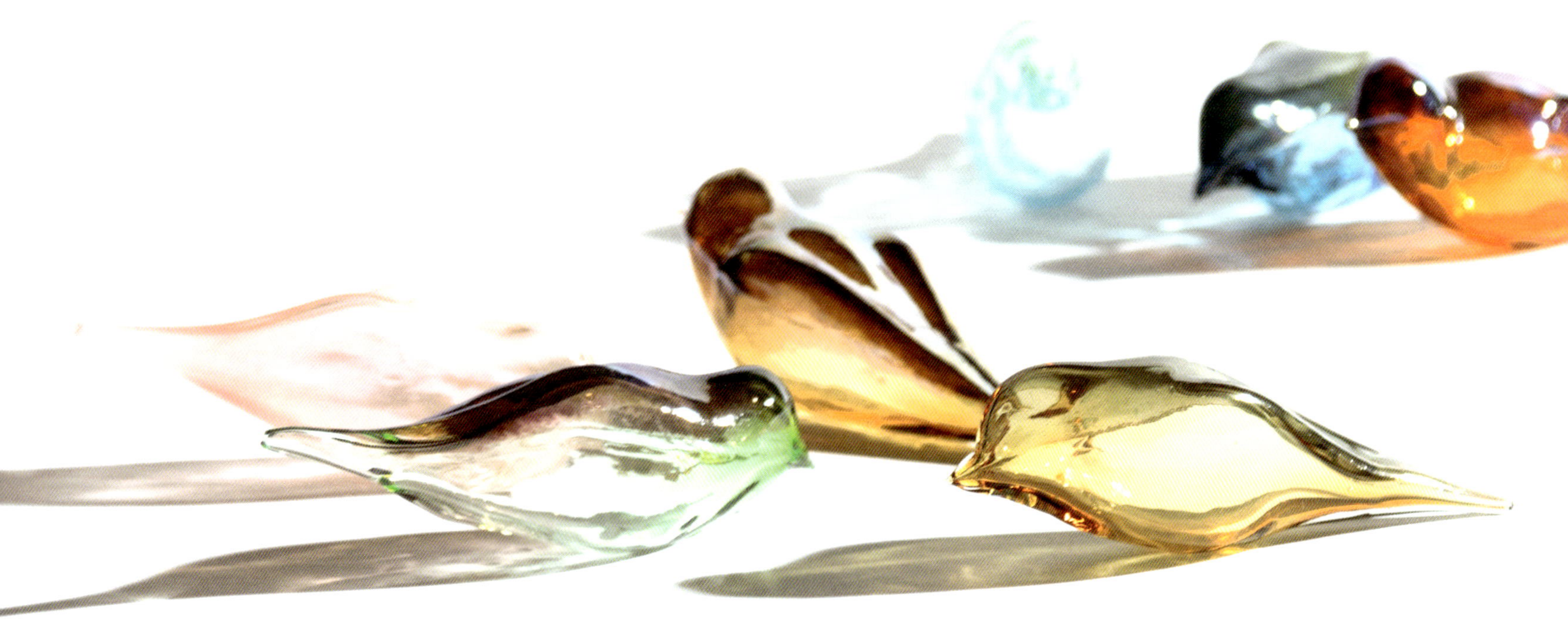

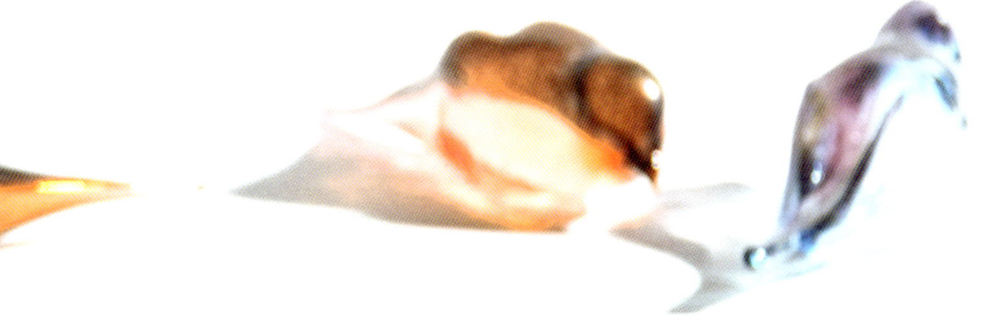

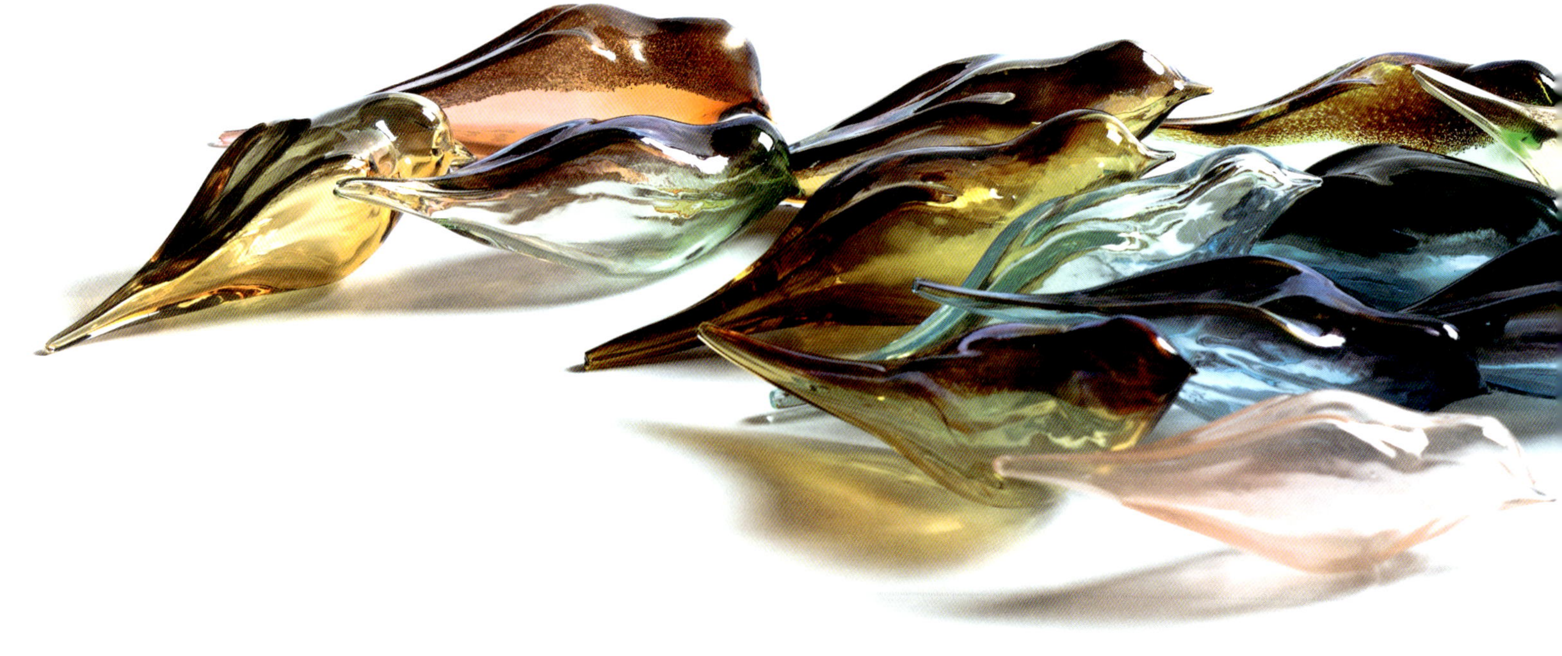

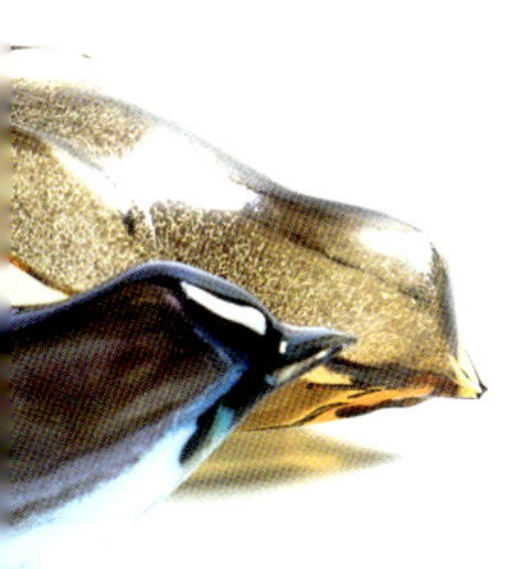

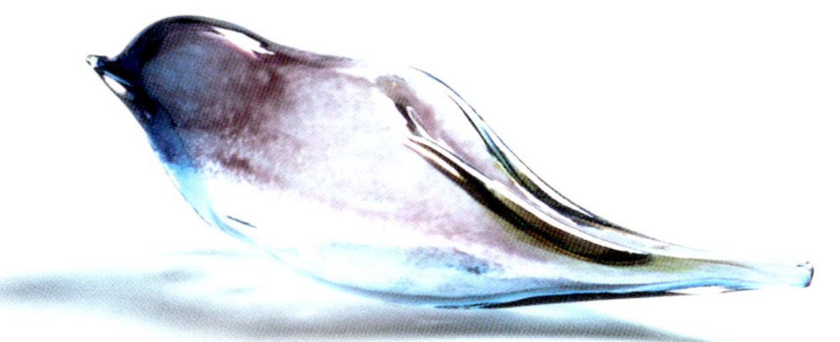

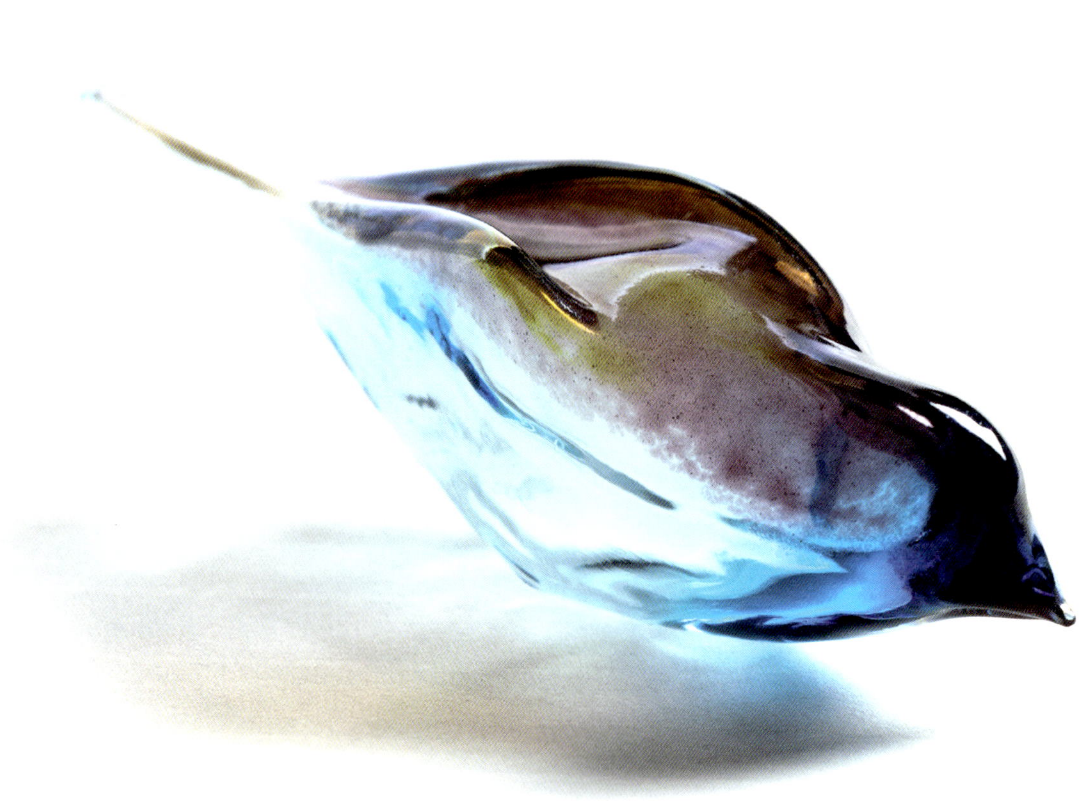

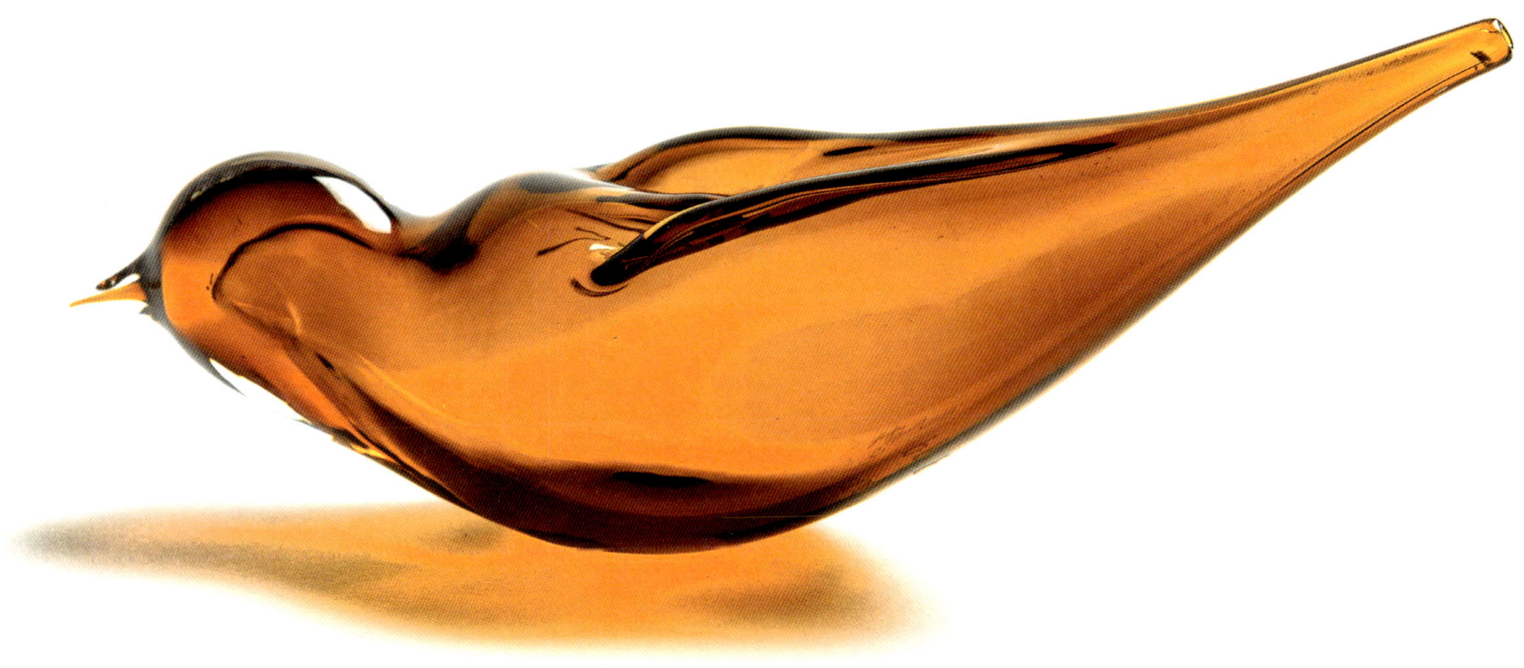

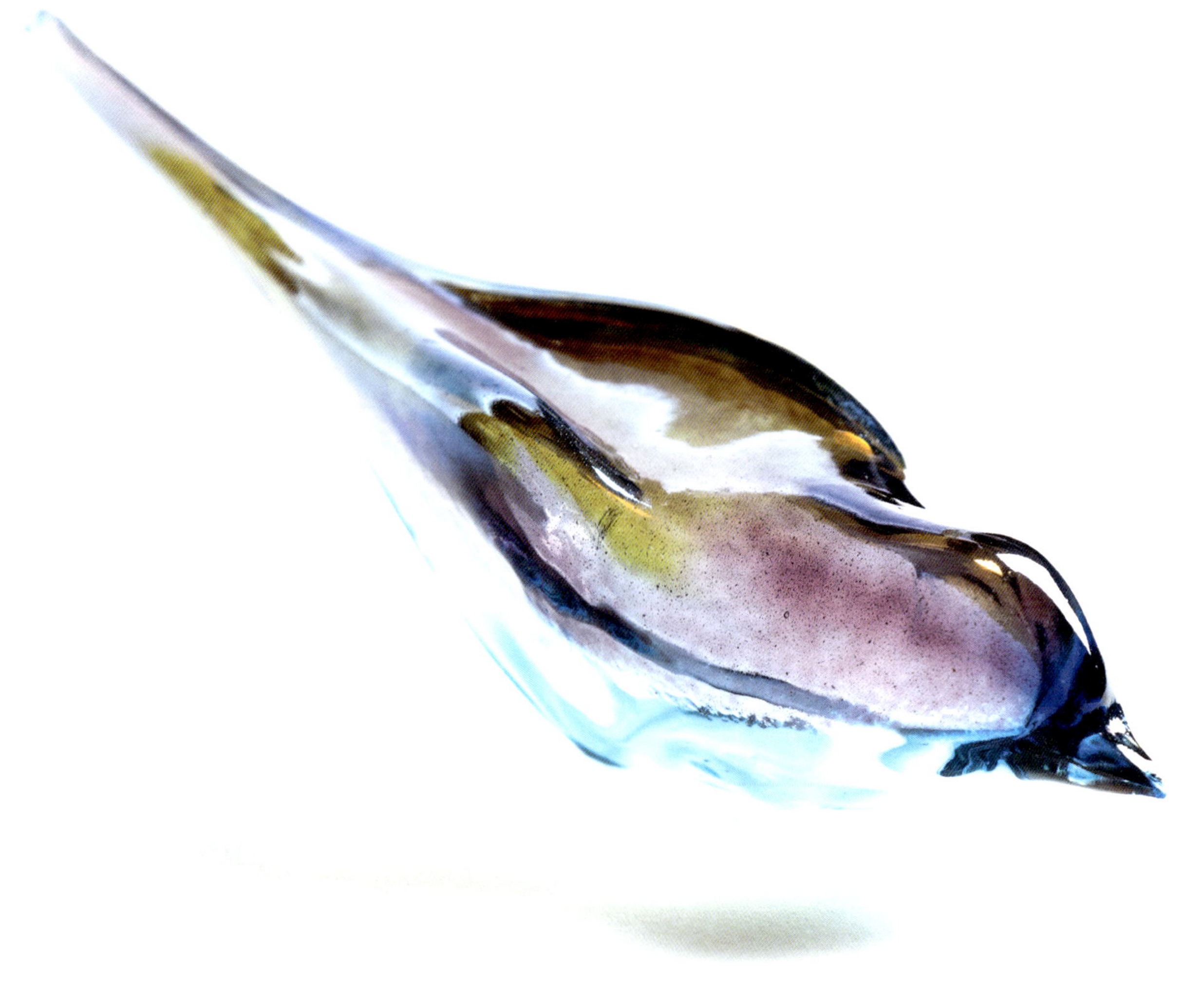

displaced

displaced

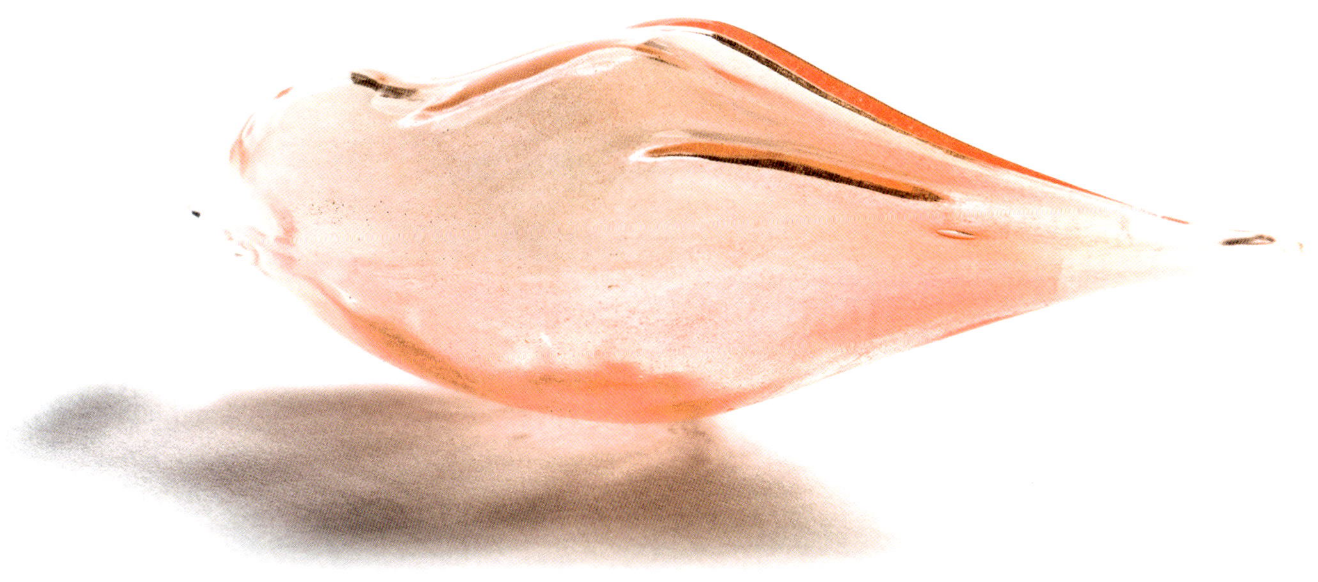

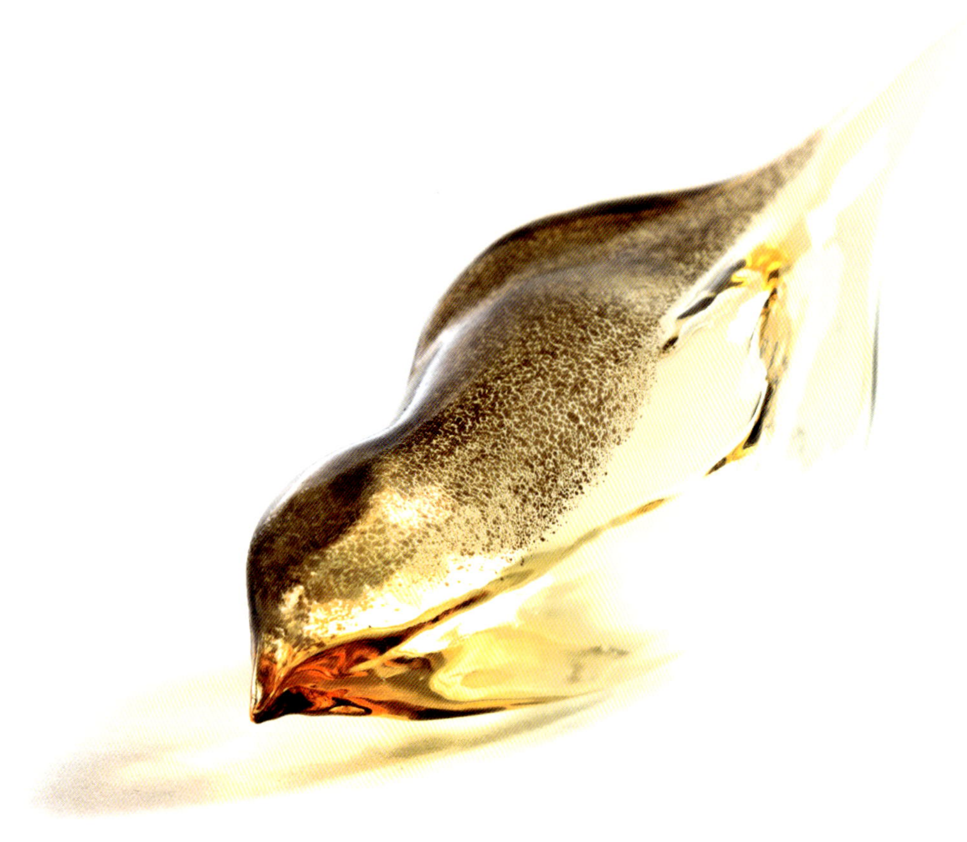

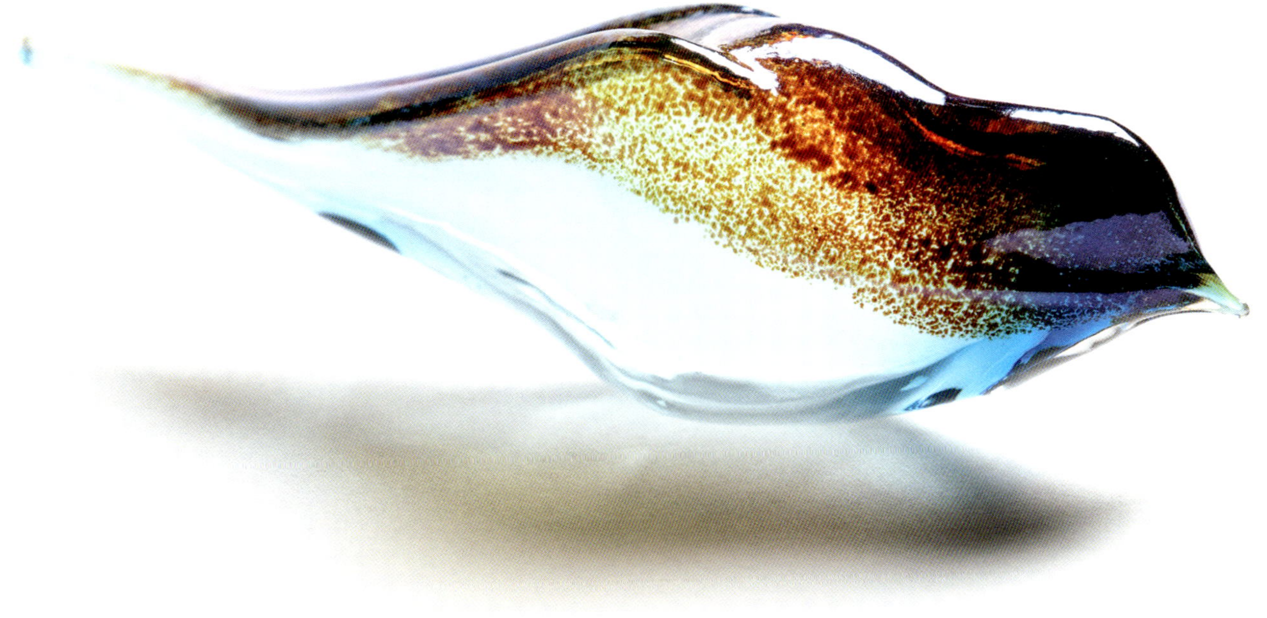

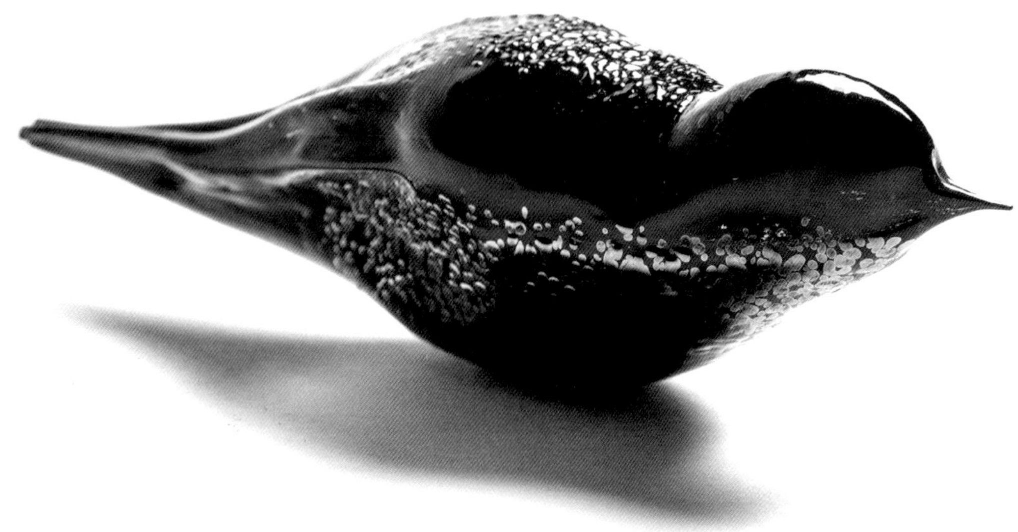

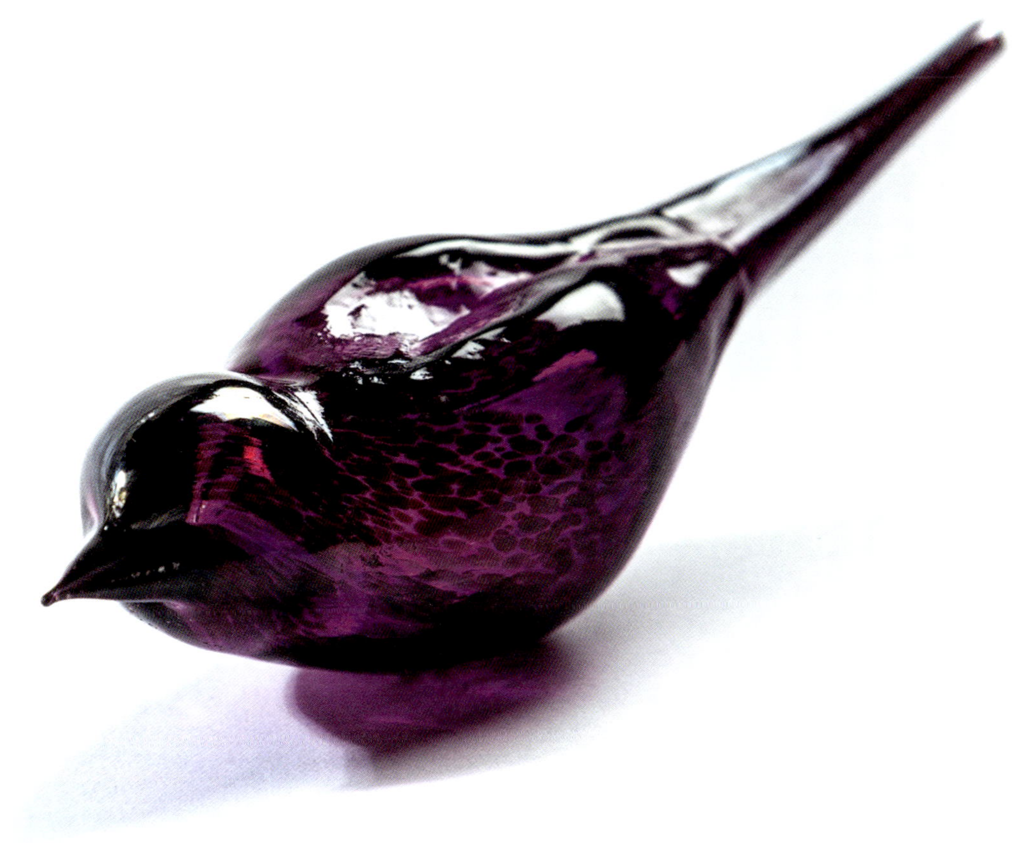

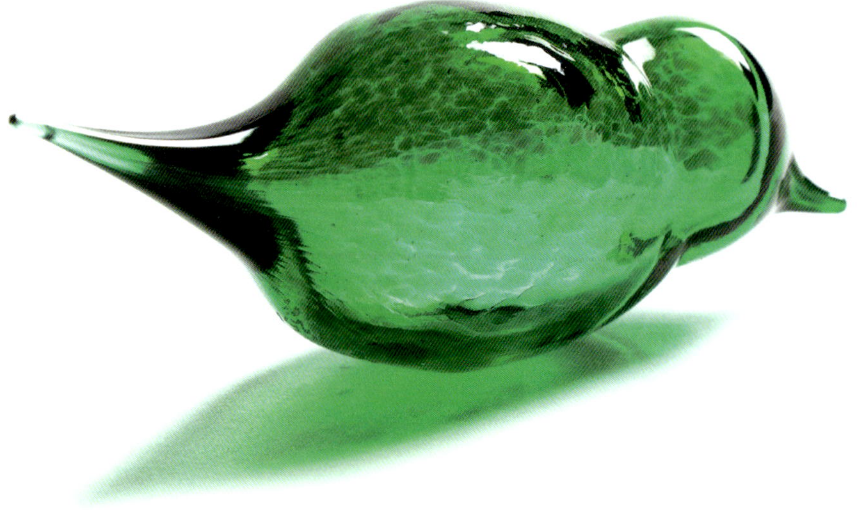

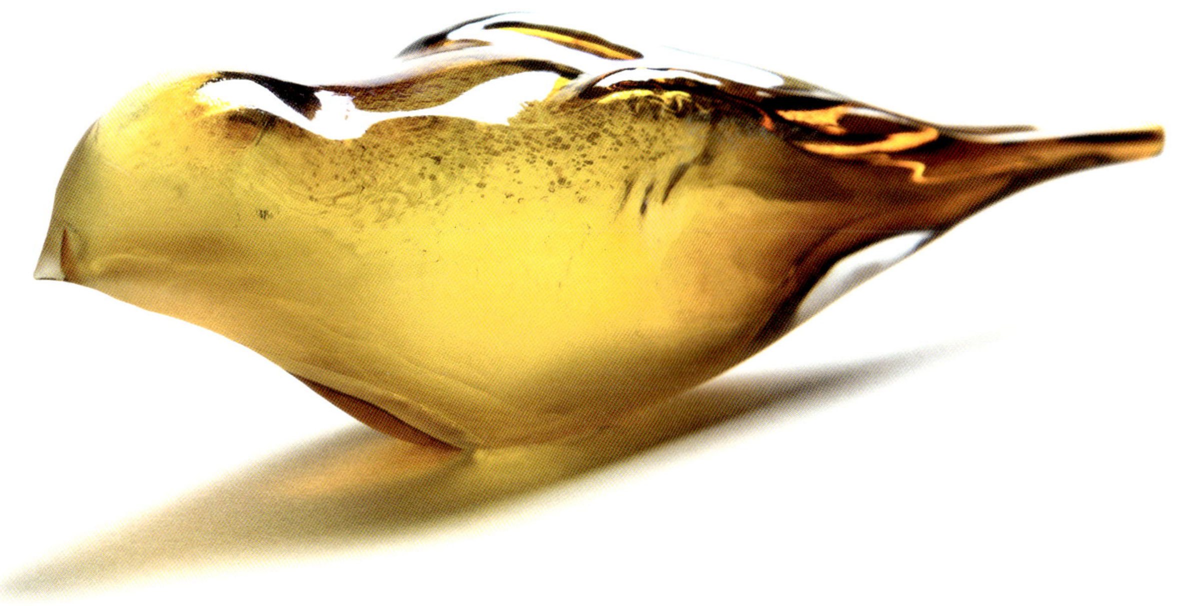

perched

betrayed

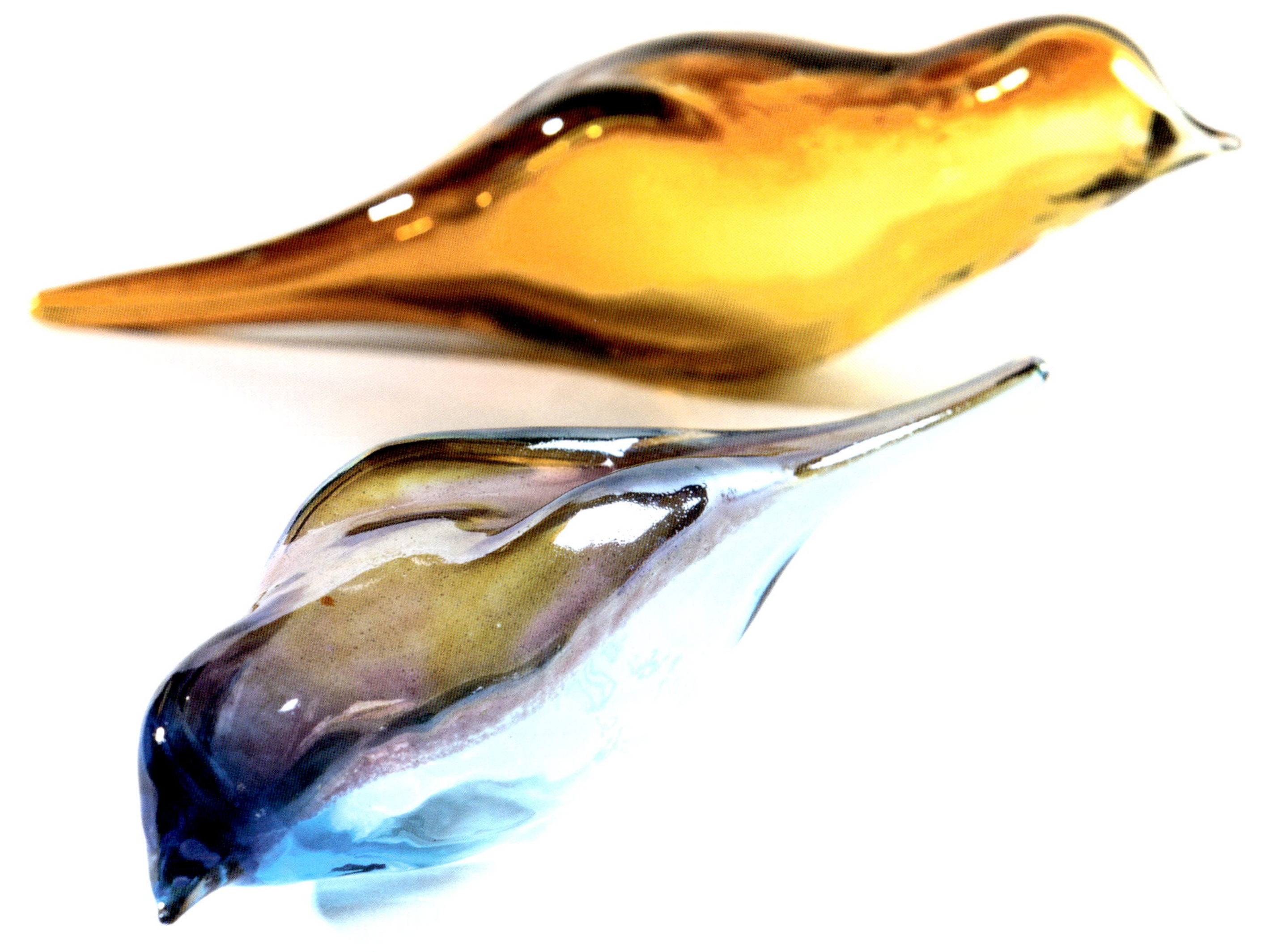

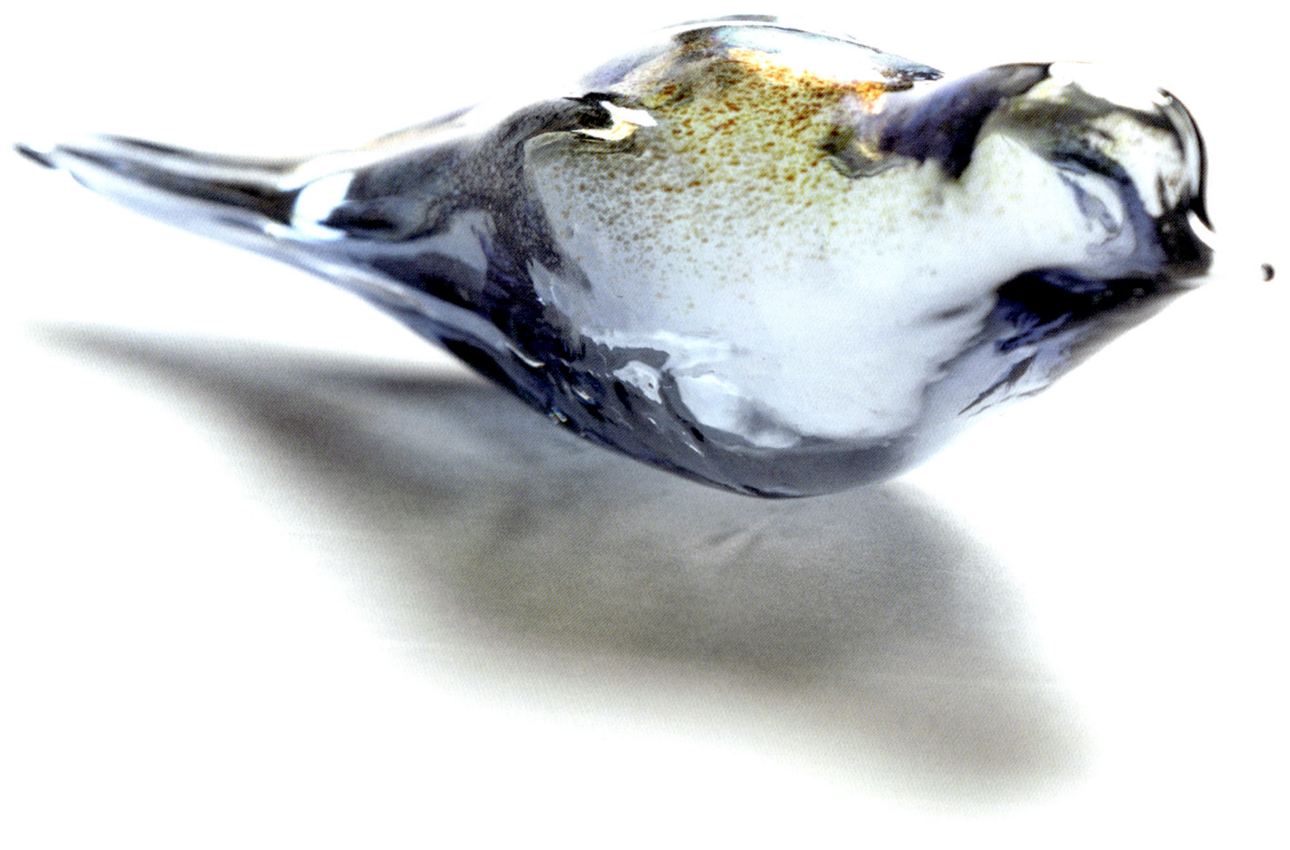

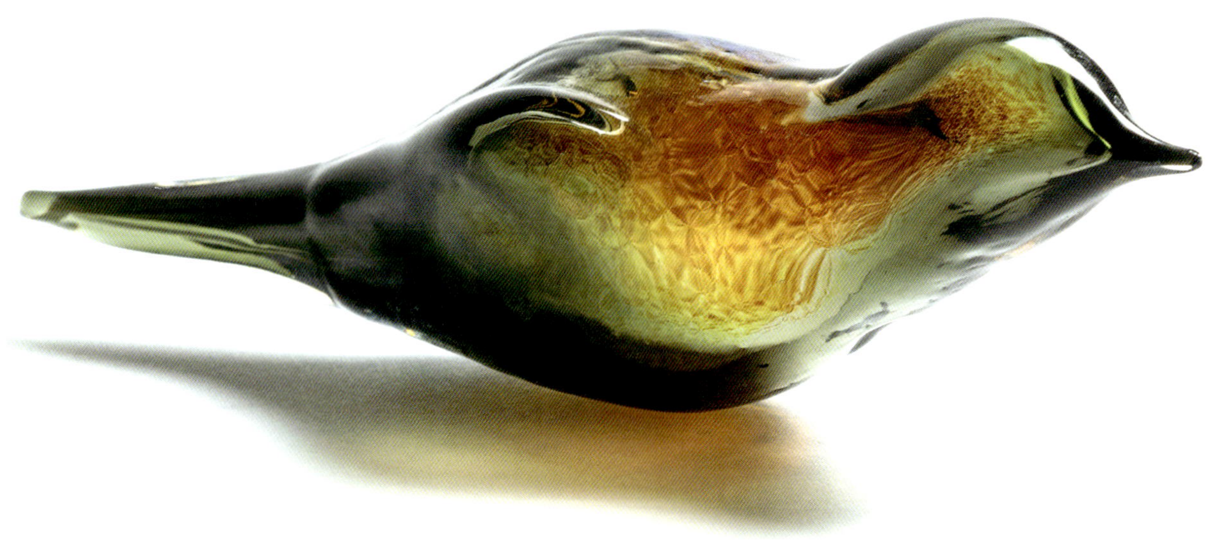

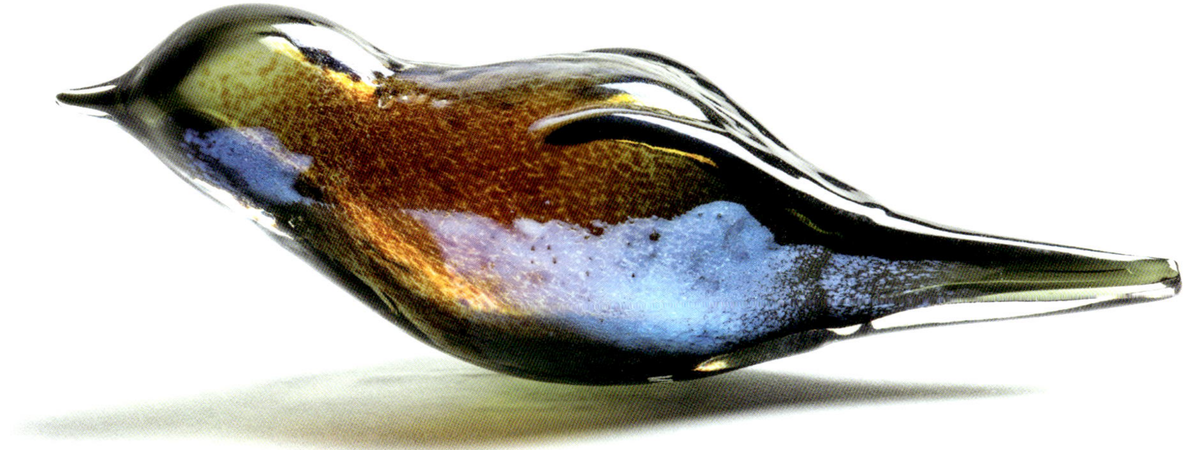

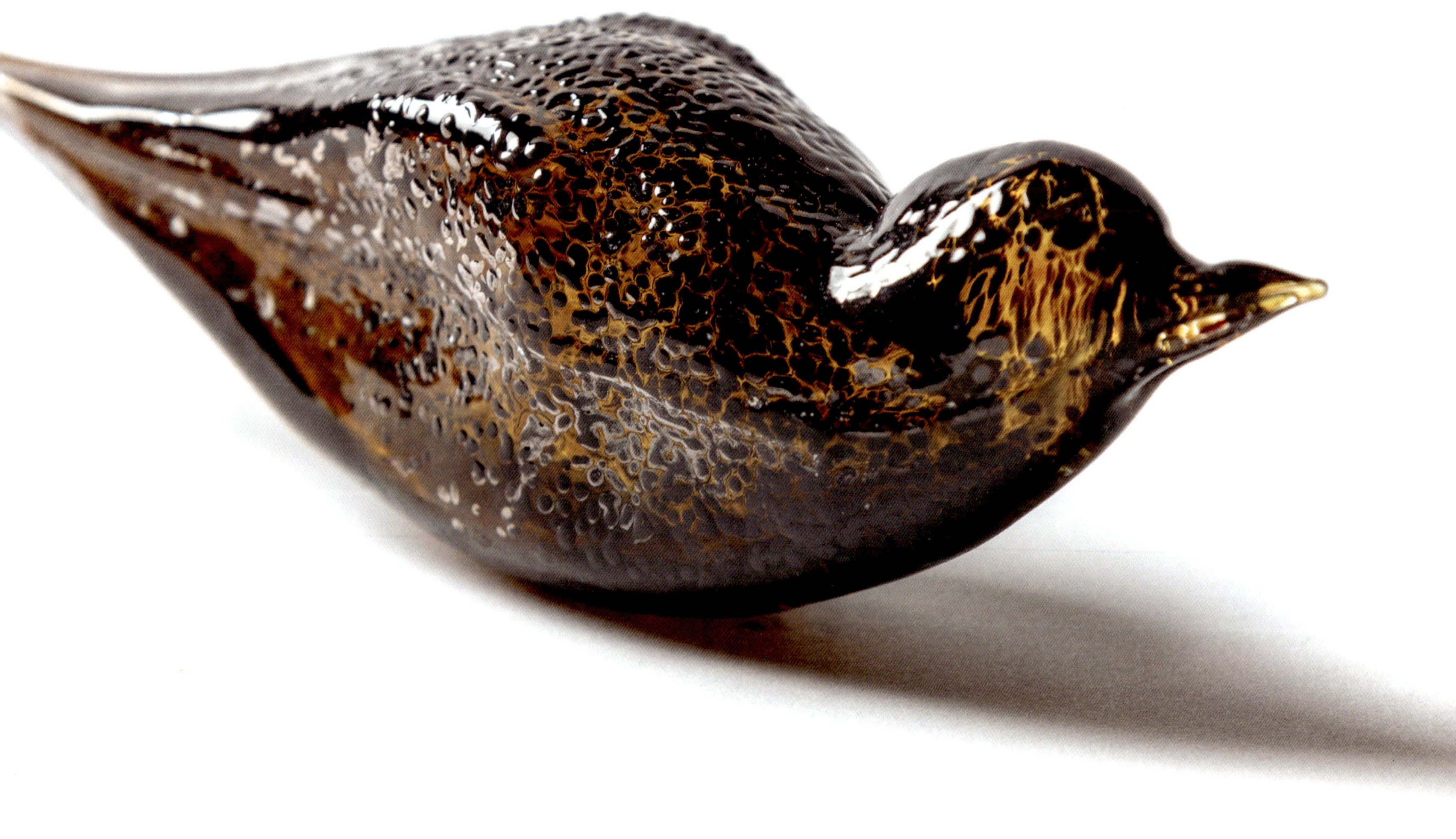

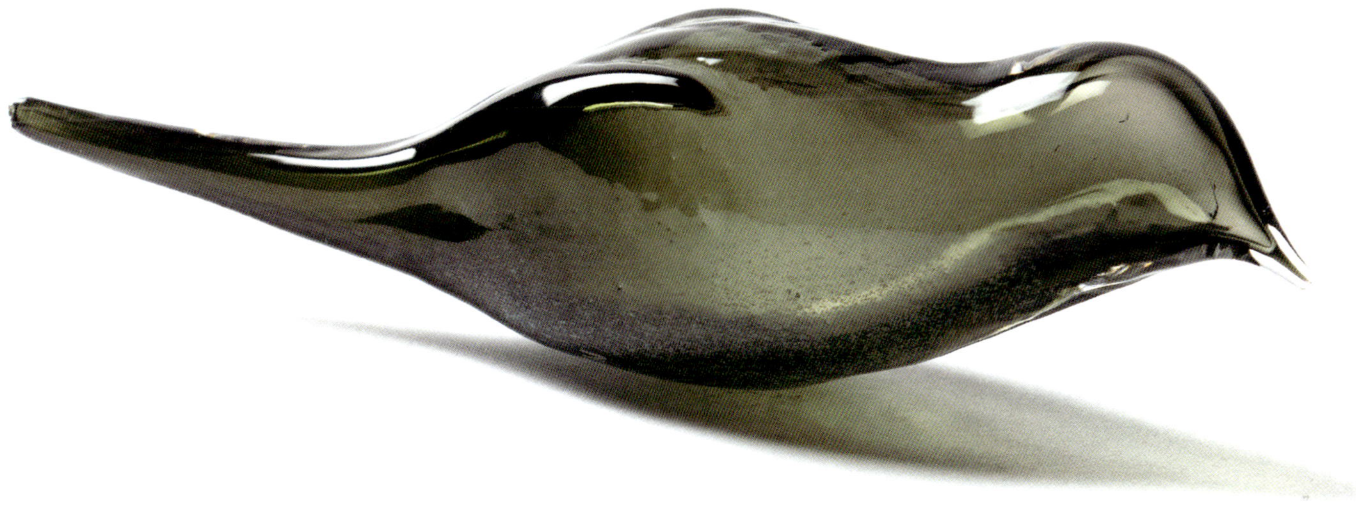

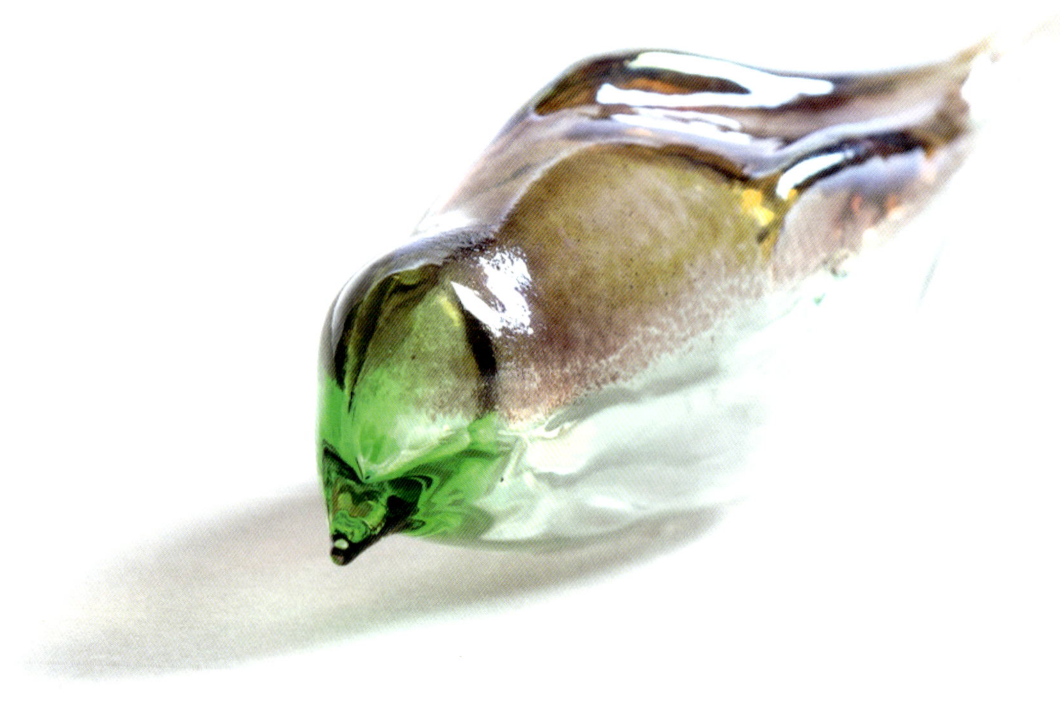

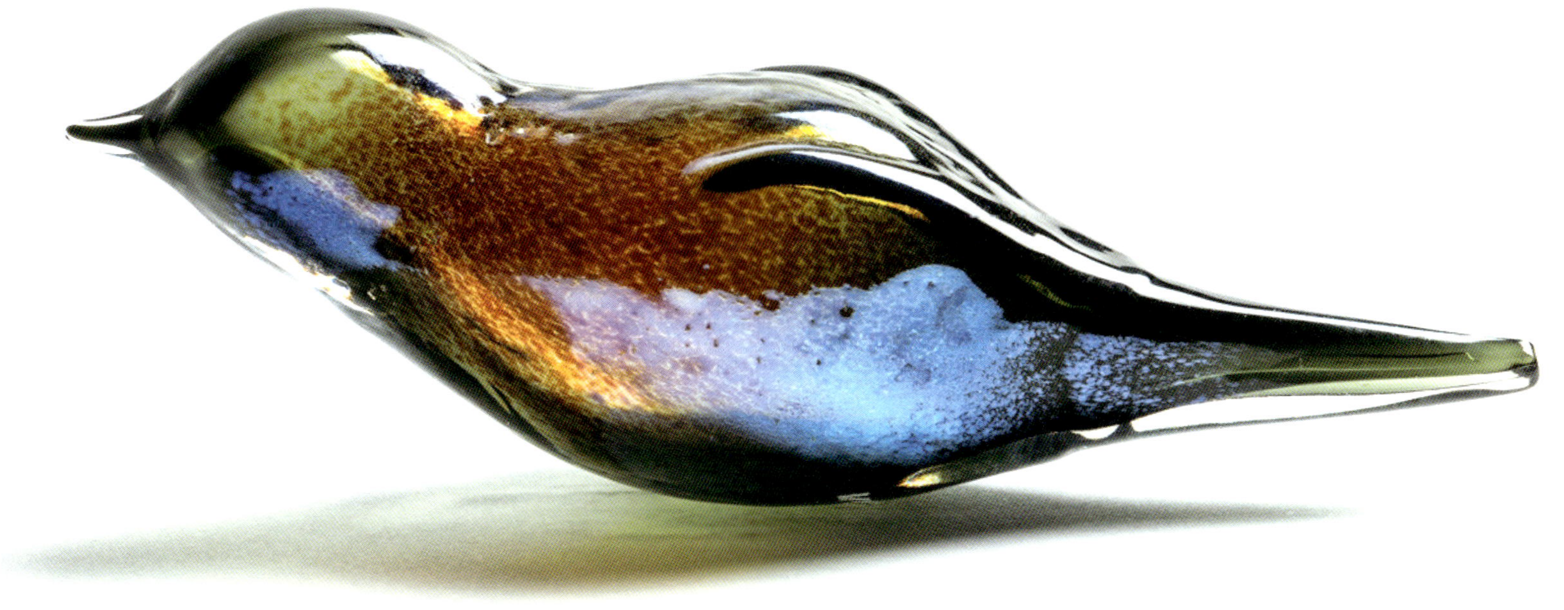

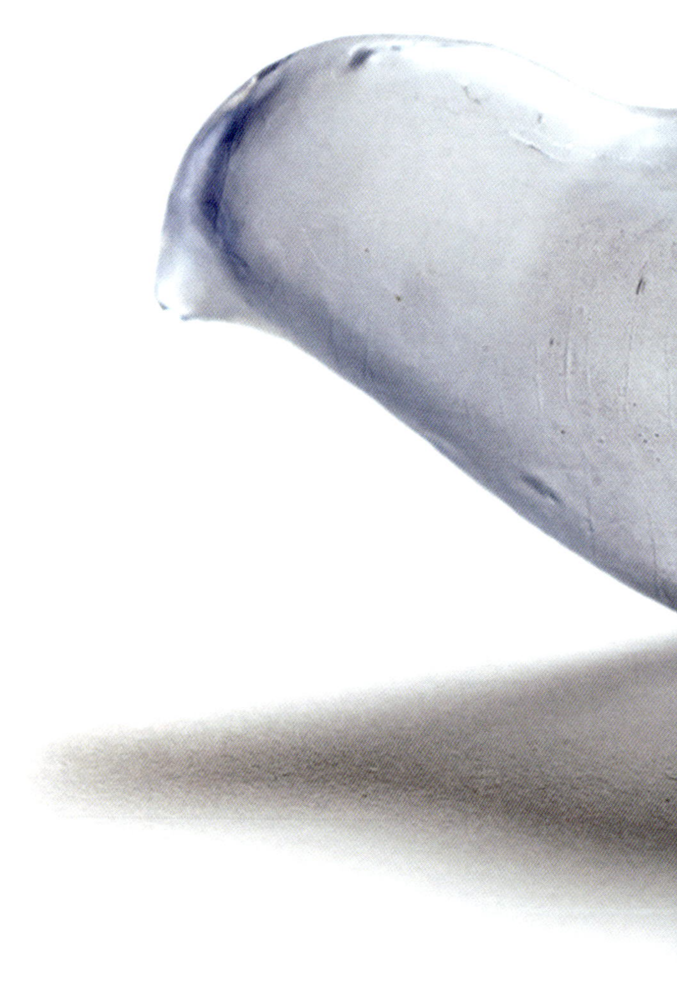

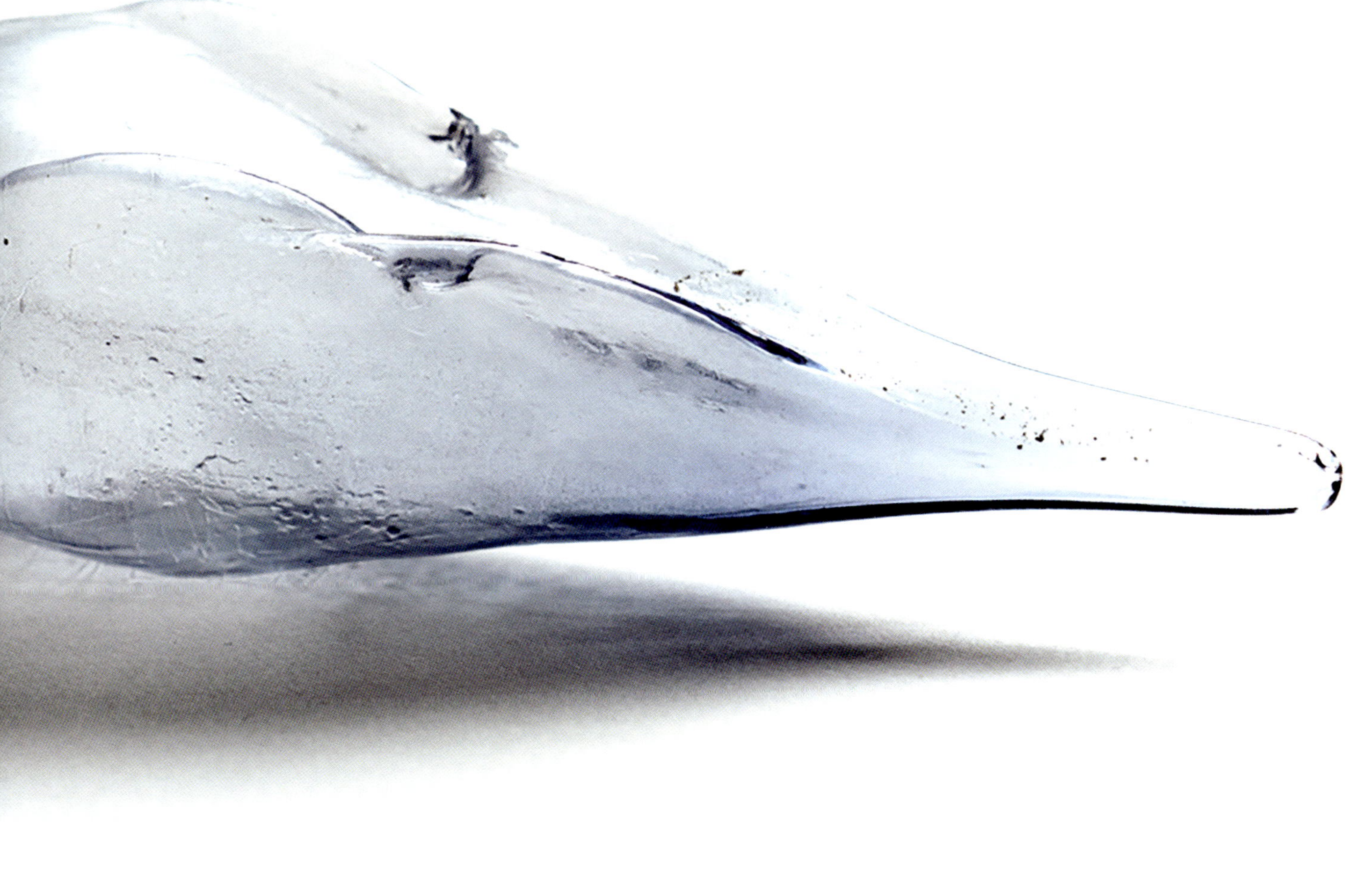

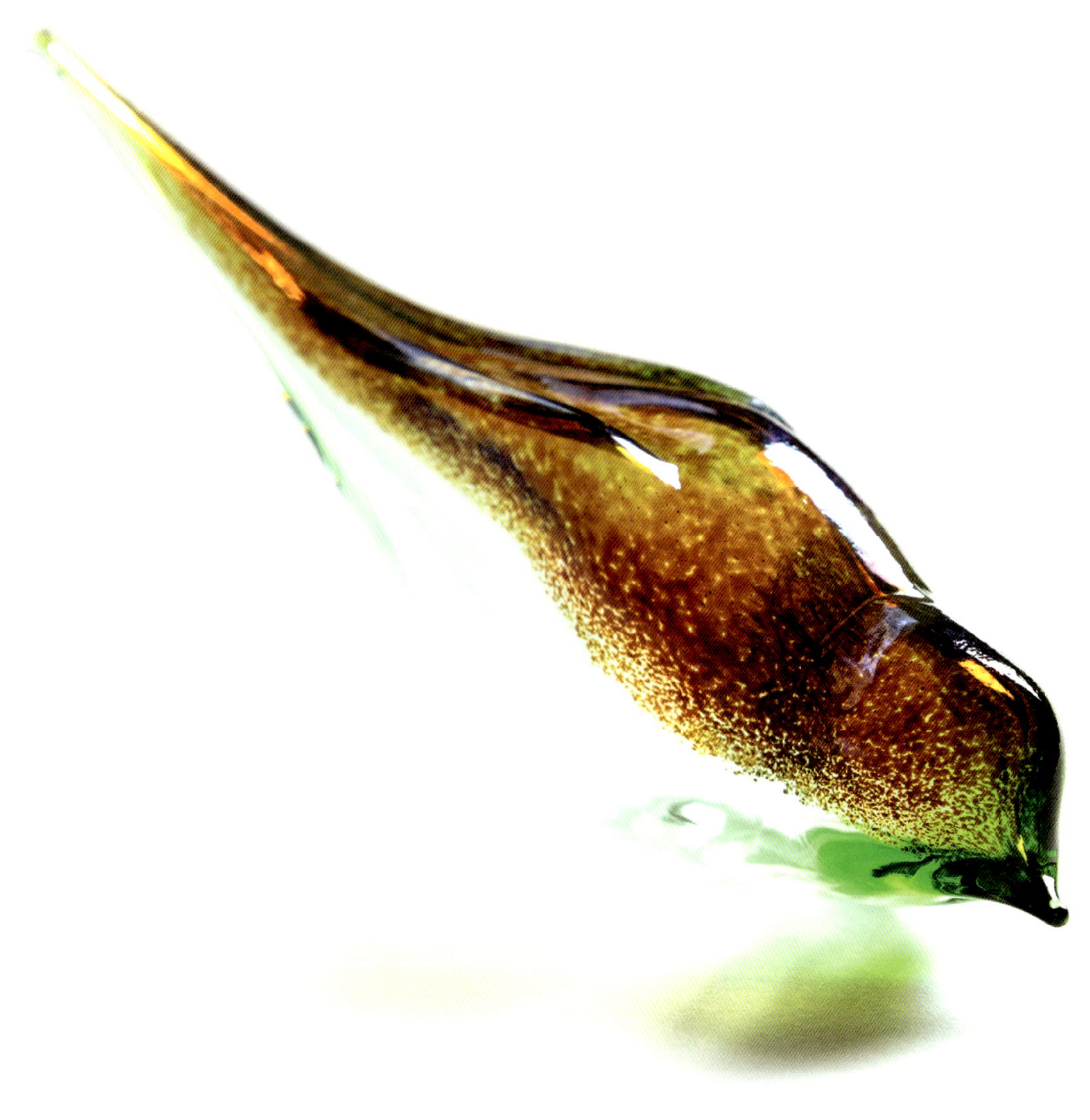

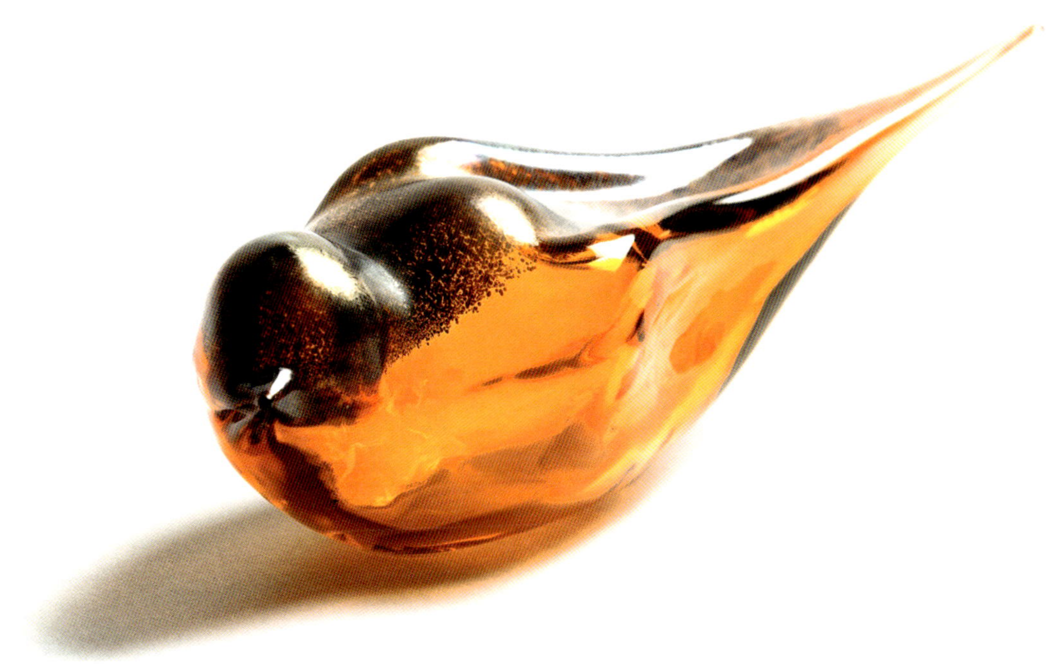

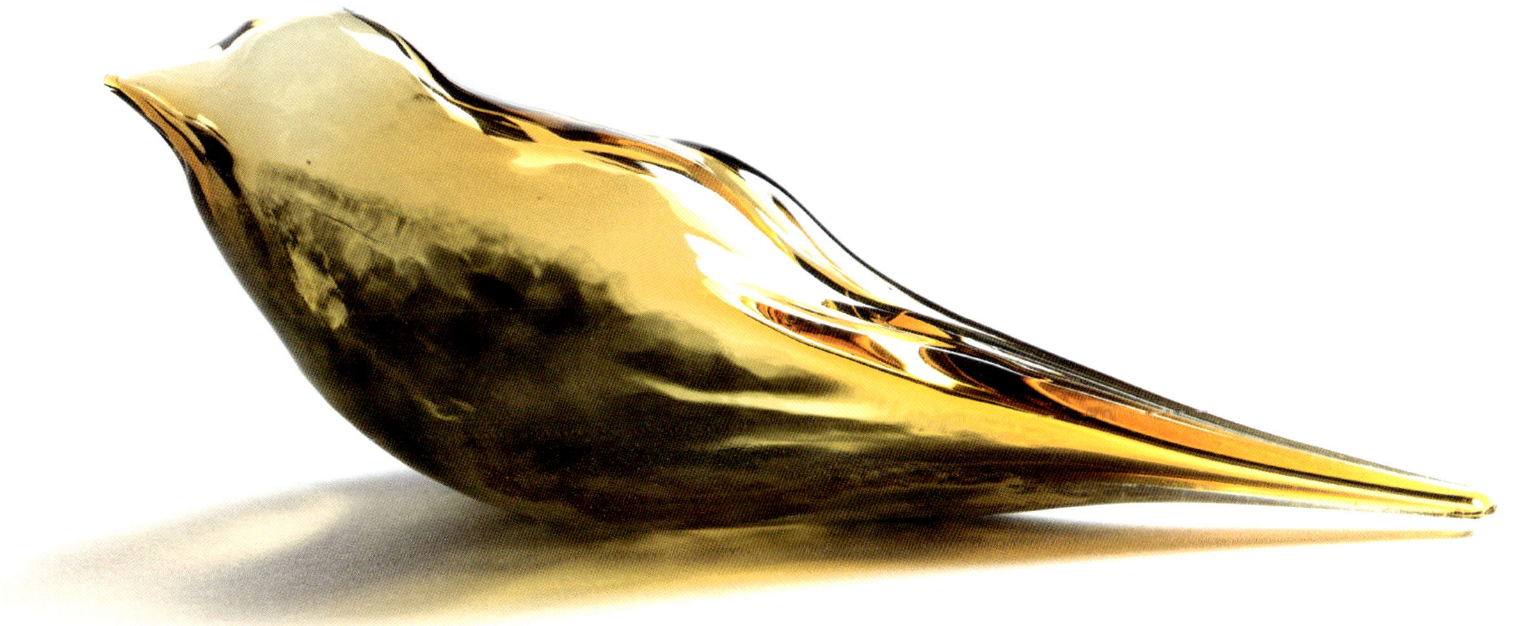

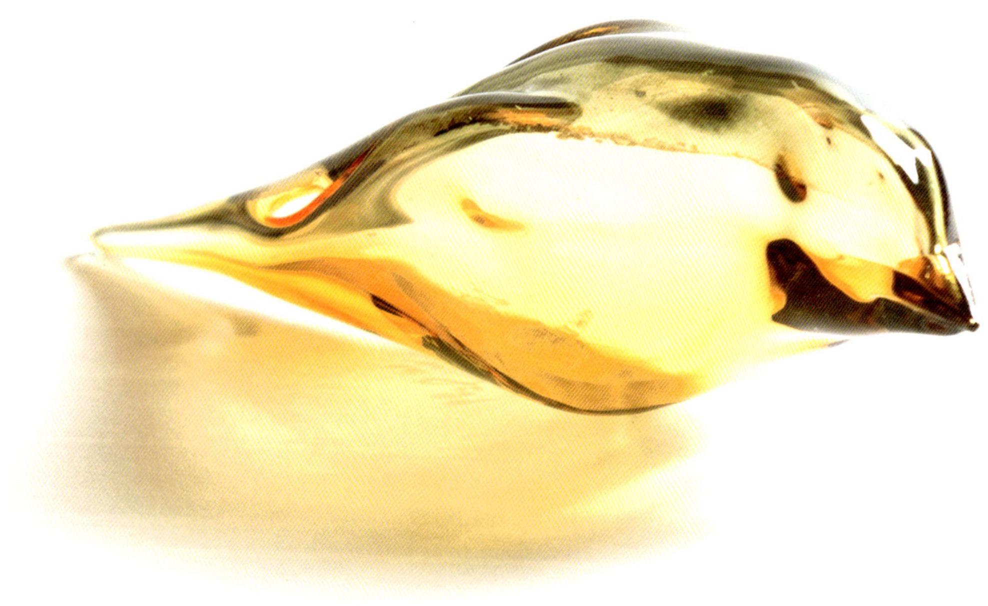

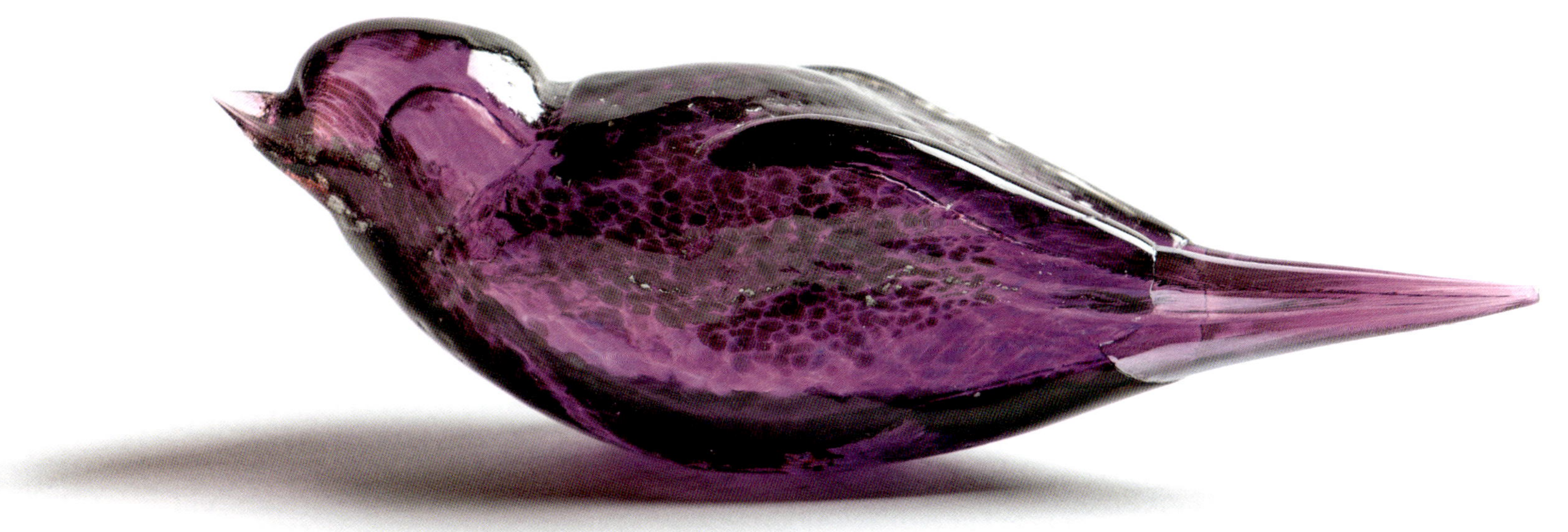

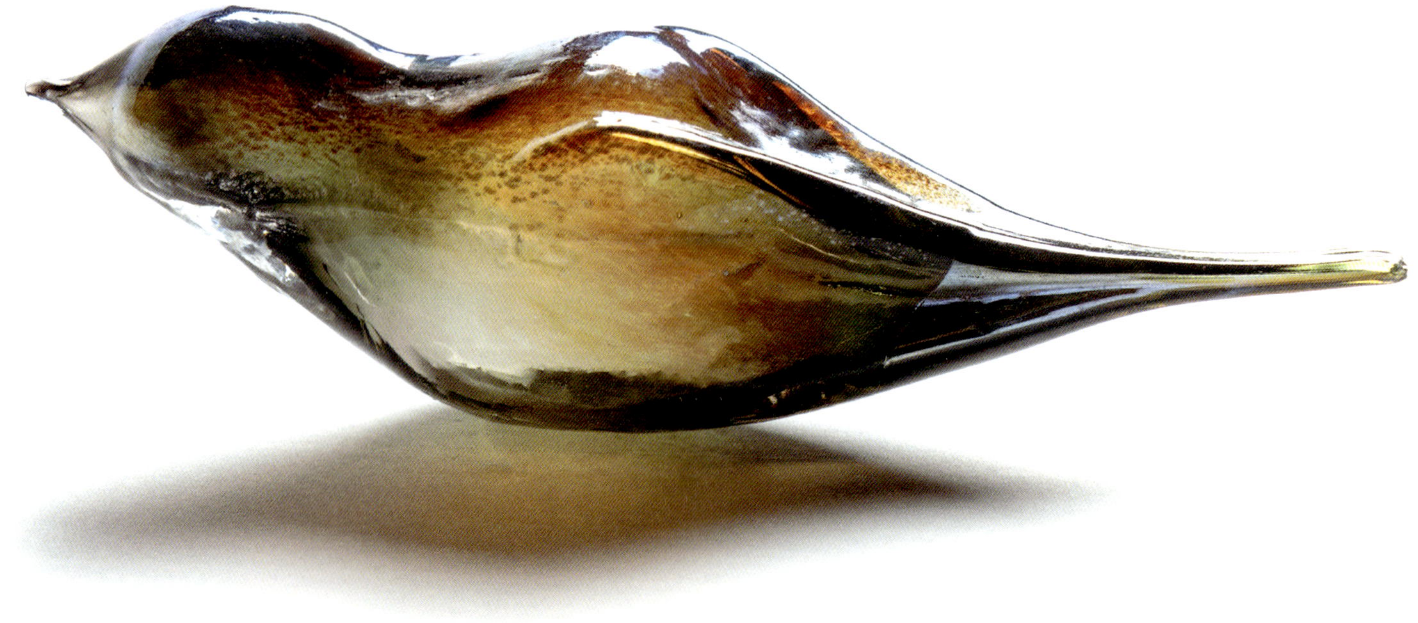

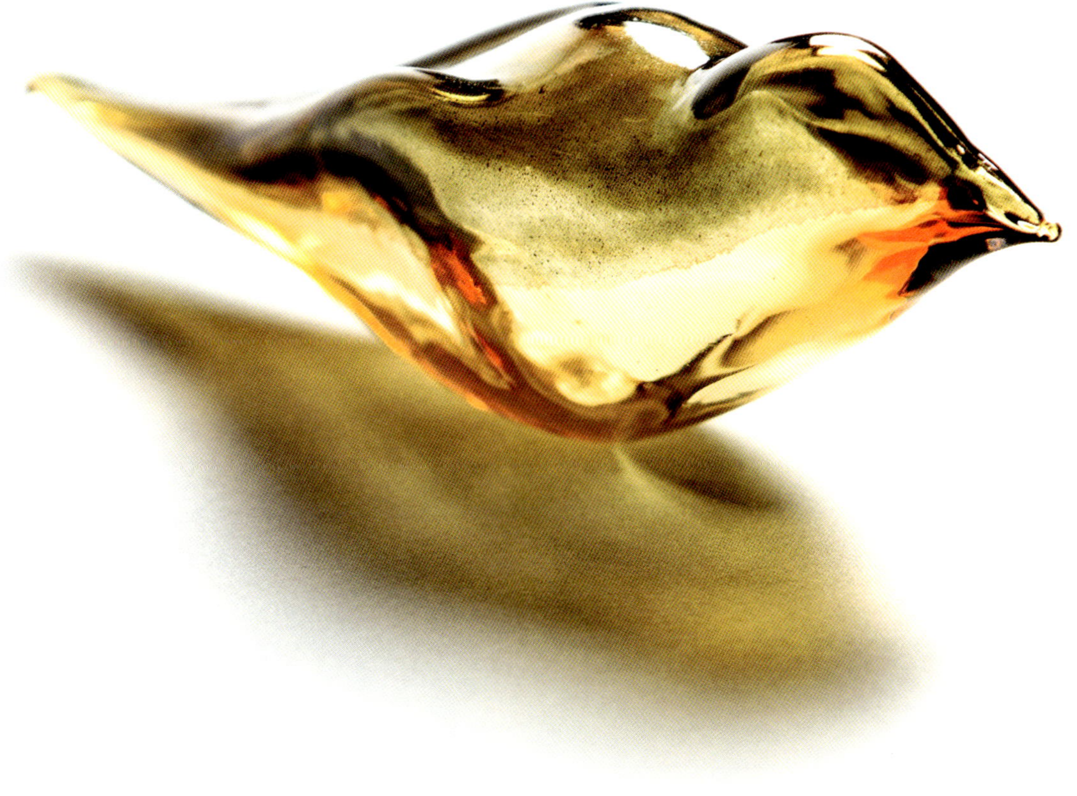

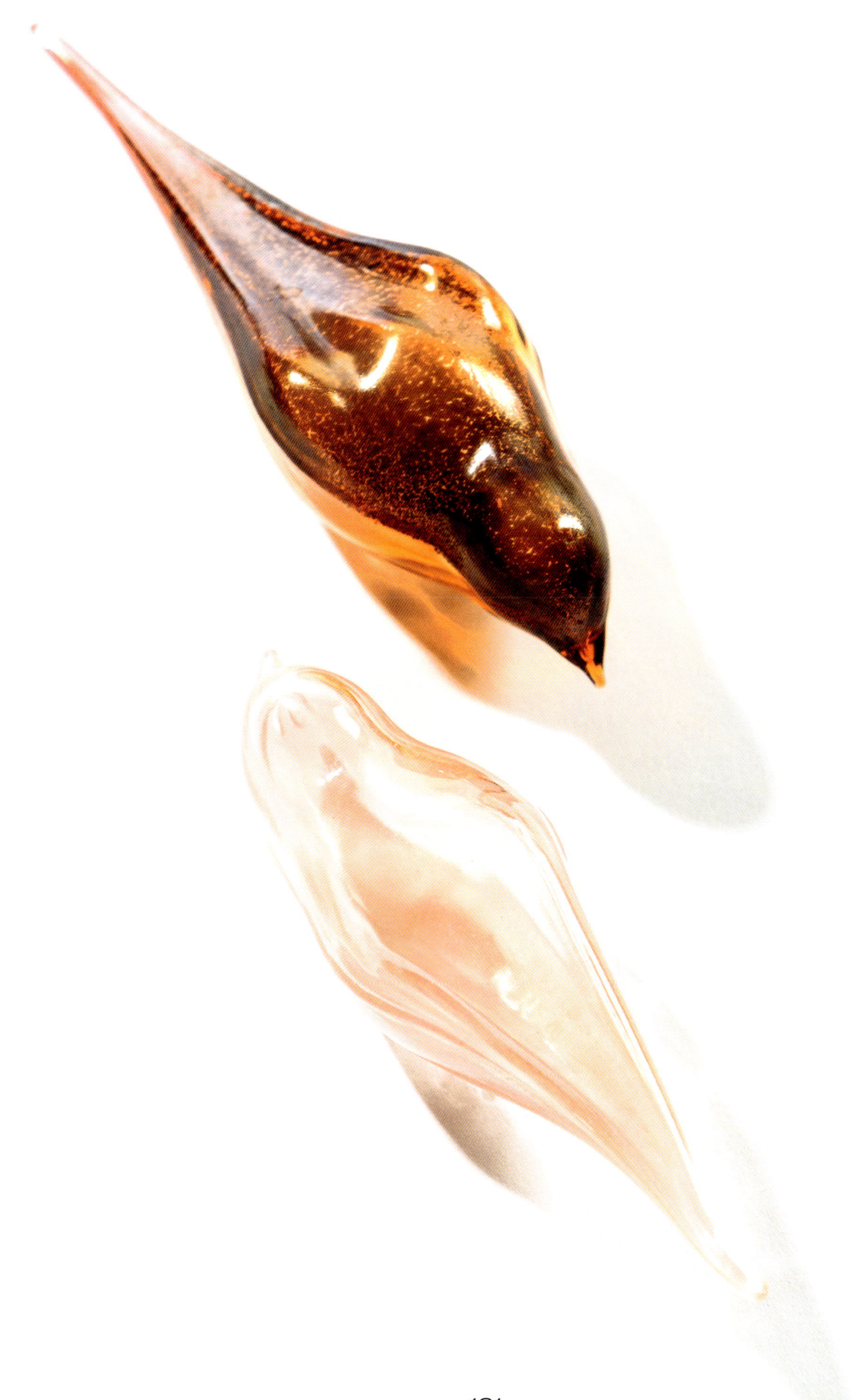

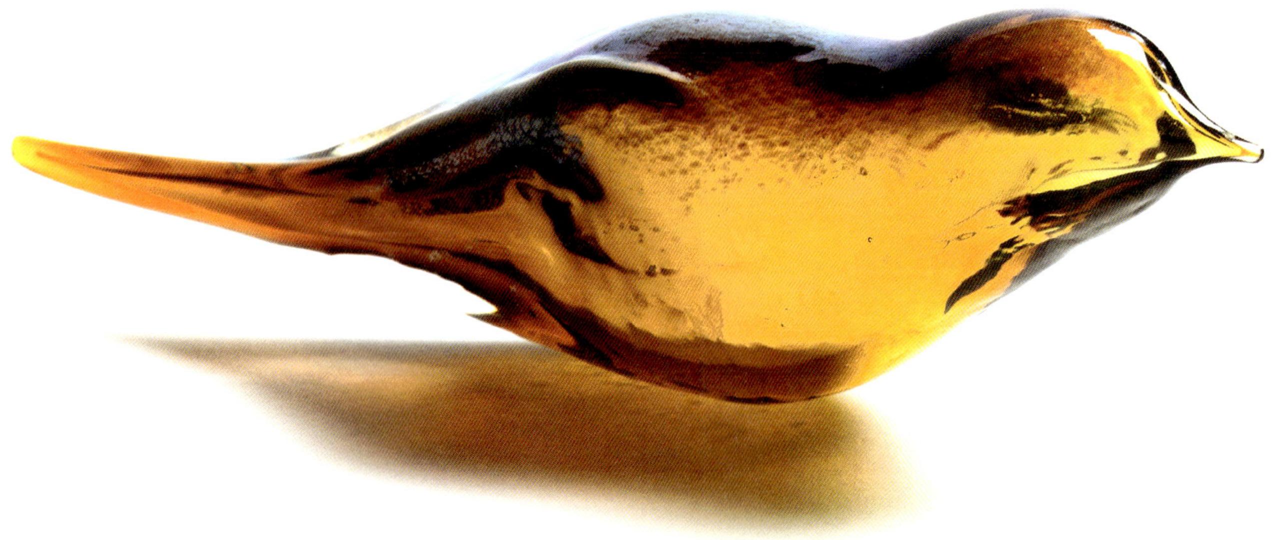

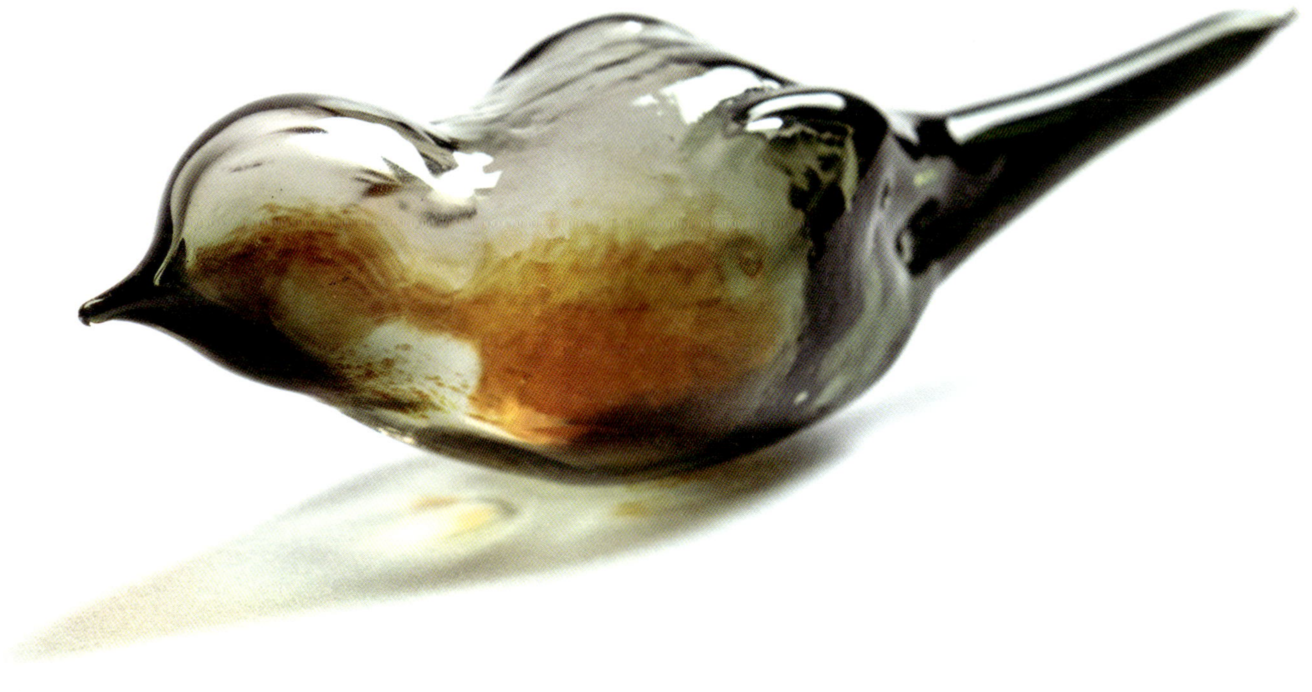

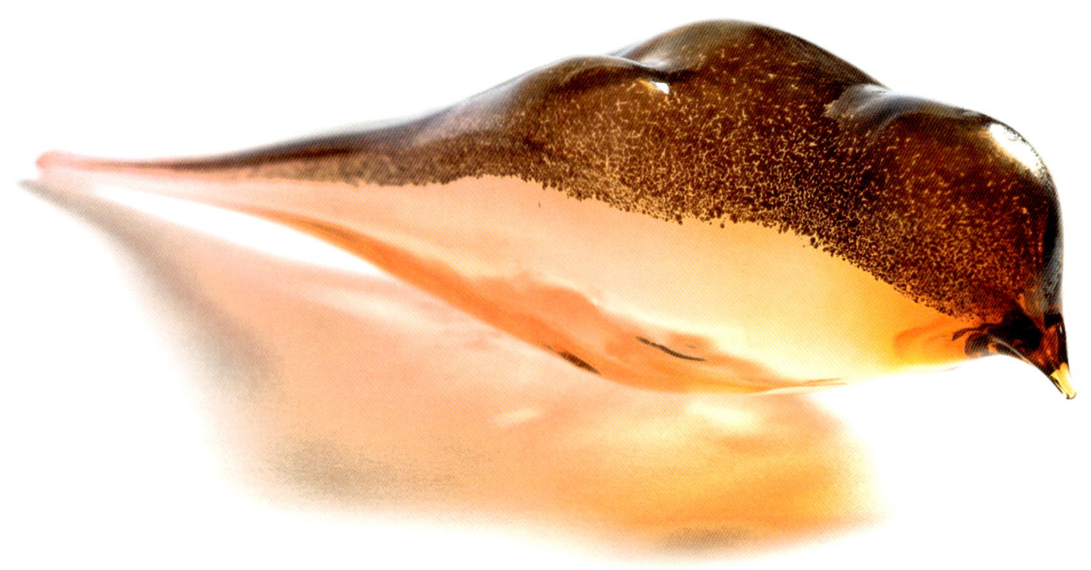

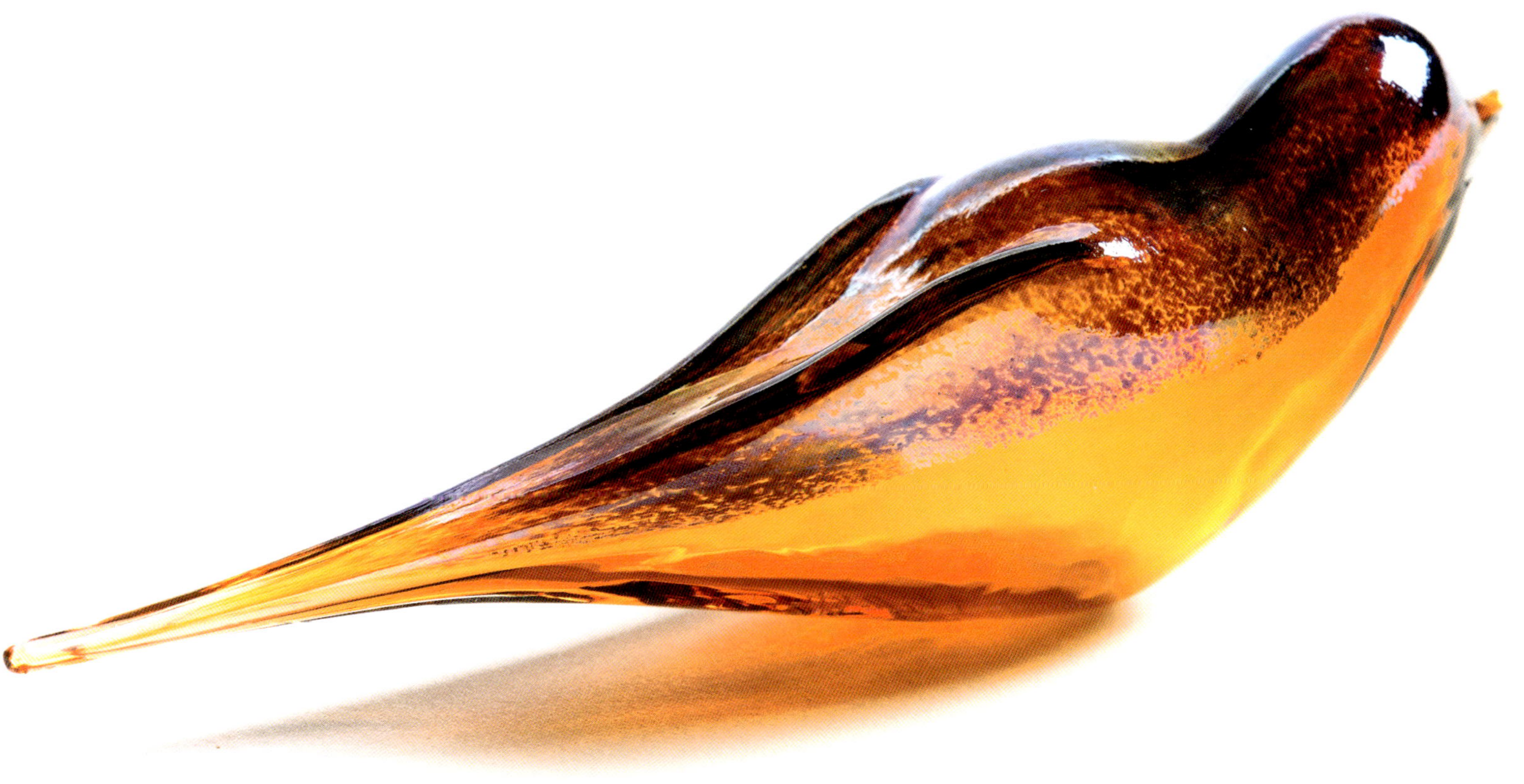

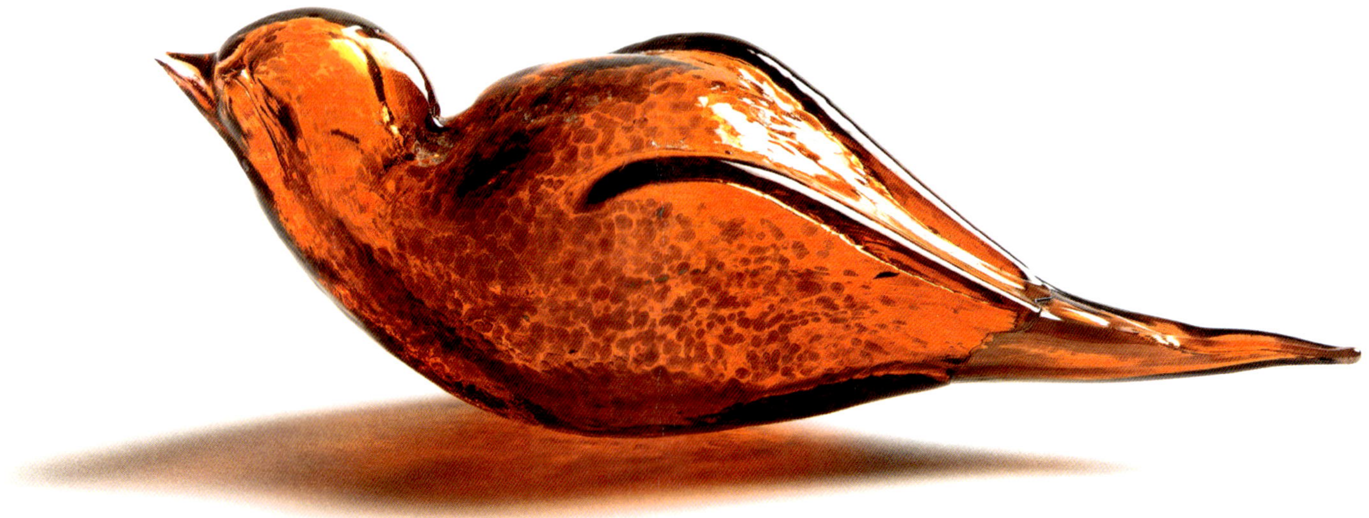

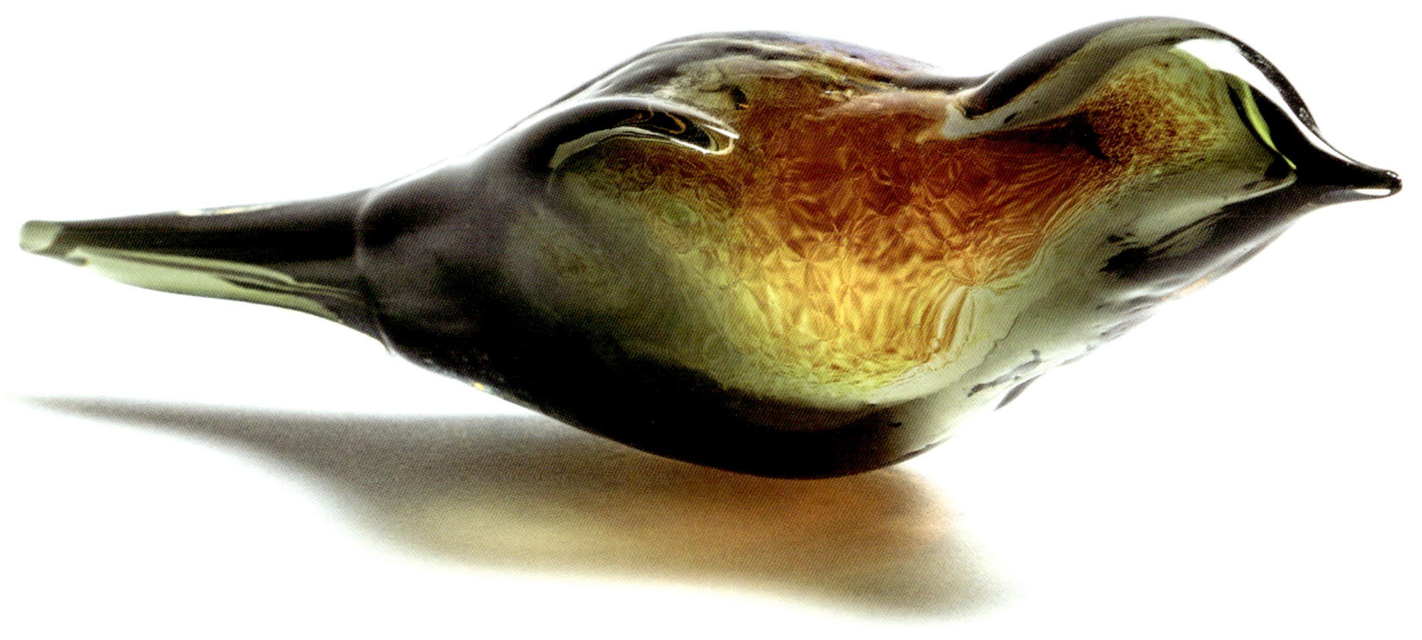

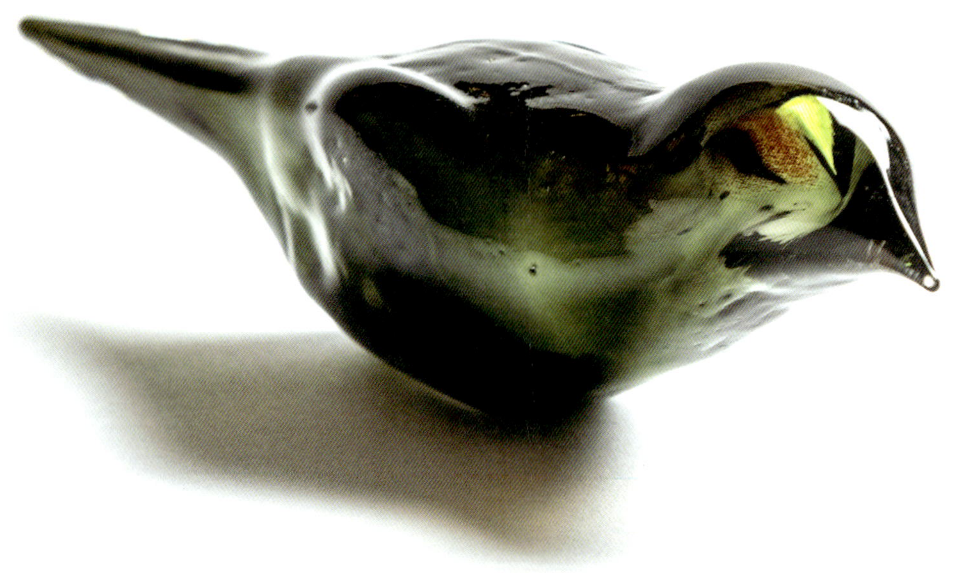

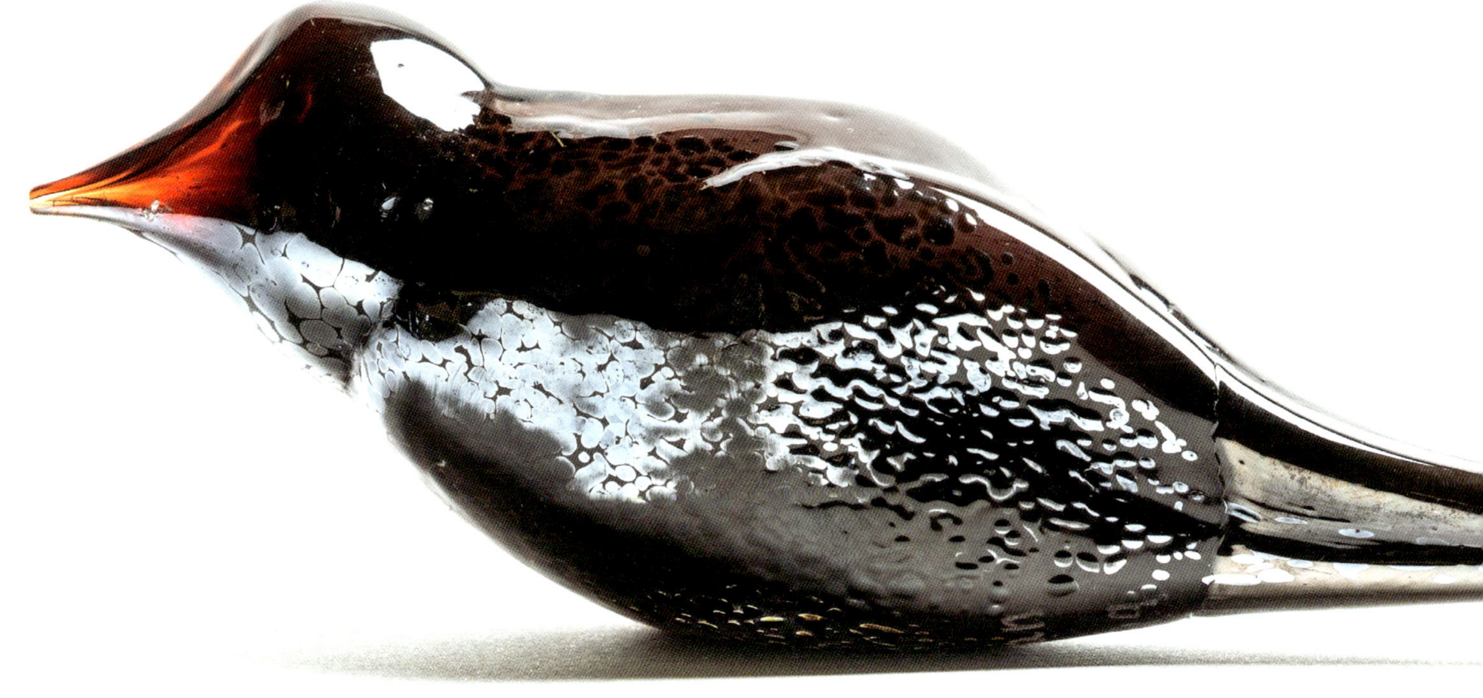

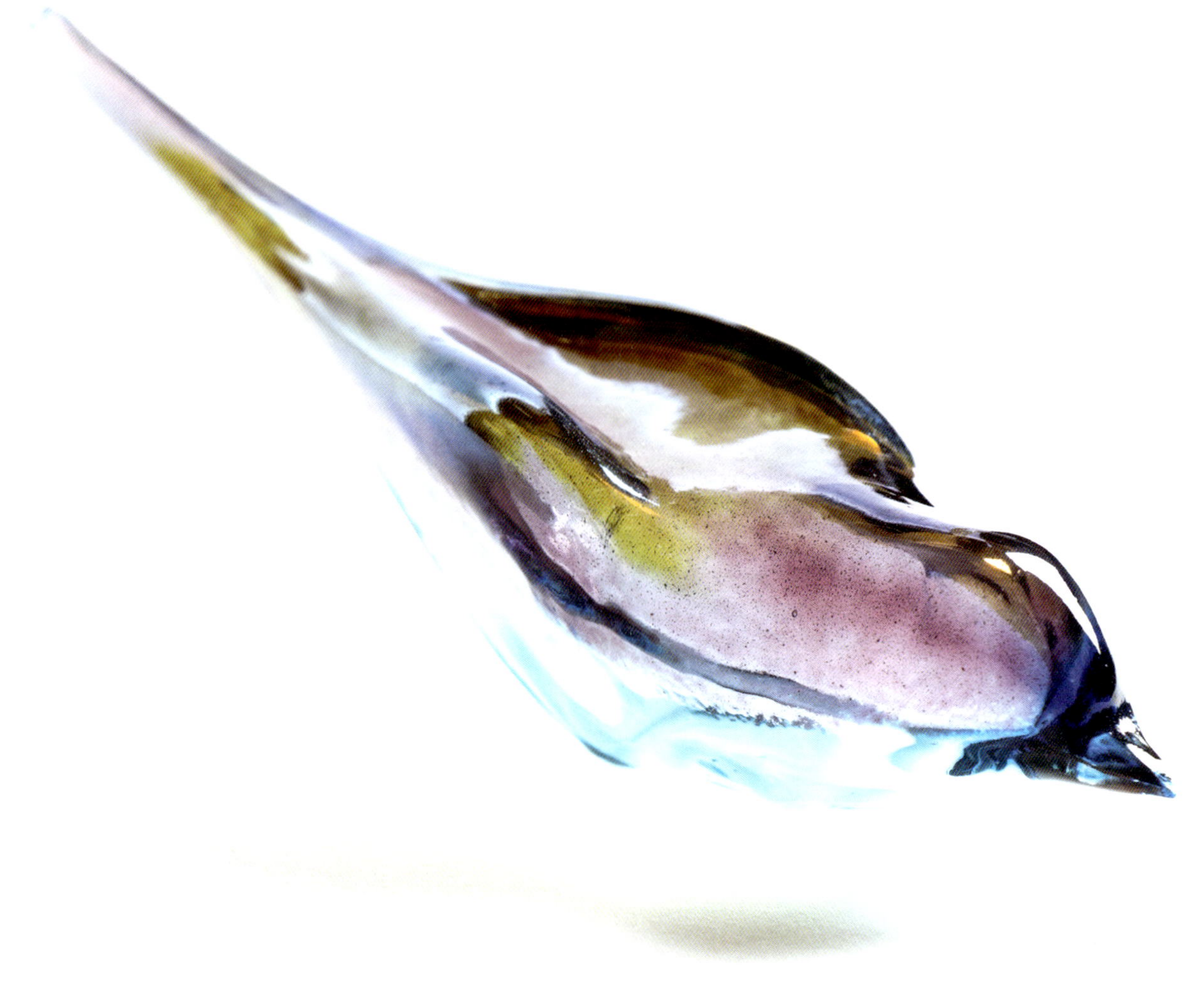

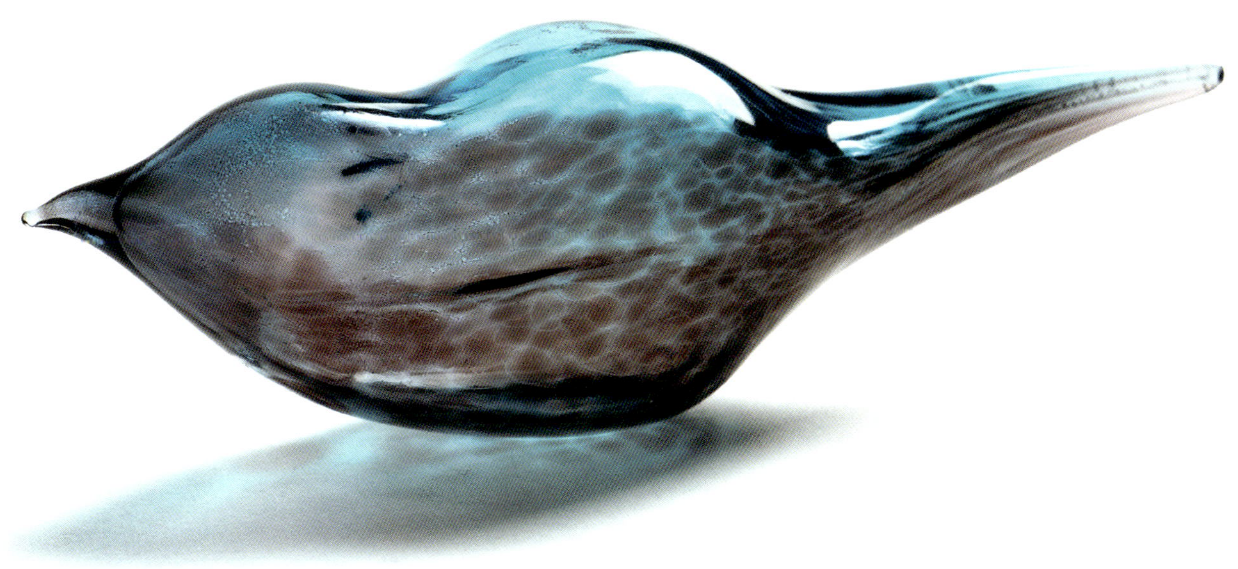

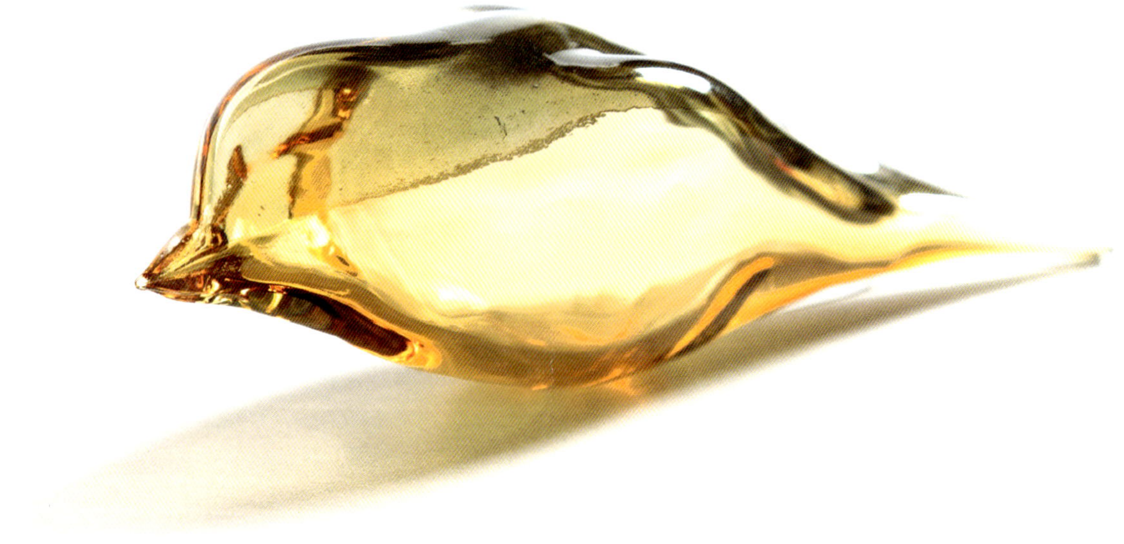

BIOGRAPHIES

FELEKŞAN ONAR

Felekşan Onar's works in glass deal with the notions of identity, constructed narratives, historical relations and impacts of politics on society, while drawing on sources from her personal history as well as collective memory. Onar particularly focuses on the cultural interaction that evolved through the art of glassmaking between different geographies. In her works, she uses several glassmaking techniques to present the amazing qualities of the material she has fallen in love with. Each piece reflects her expertise in the glassmaking techniques of blowing, casting and fusing and mirror the sense of lightness and grace by translating the simple and skilful aesthetic into glass. Producing glass art, to use her own words, "not only expresses my past and present, but also my anxieties and expectations for future. Through glass, I speak, breathe and live."

Felekşan Onar completed her undergraduate degree in Economics and Music History at Cornell University and undertook further studies at Harvard Business School. She started off in a private atelier and later on received her formal education in glass at Glass Furnace, Istanbul. In 2003, she started her own atelier, Fy-Shan Glass Studio, which designs and produces limited-edition functional glass art, objects and lighting. In her studio, she collaborates internationally with design brands, architects, interior designers and design galleries to create special collections and commissions.

Recent solo shows include *Perched*, Victoria and Albert Museum, London (2019); *41X*, Palazzo Contarini Polignac, Venice (2018); *Perched. An installation from Felekşan Onar*, Pergamon Museum, Berlin (2018); group exhibitions include *Oh, What a World! What a World!*, New Jersey Visual Arts Center, New York (2018); and *1001 Nights*, Arkas Art Center, Izmir (2018). Her works are included in international collections such as; Victoria & Albert Museum (London), Pergamon Museum (Berlin), and The Finnish Glass Museum (Riihimäki), among others as well as in local and private collections. Onar lives and works in Istanbul.

GLENN ADAMSON

is a curator, writer and historian who works on the intersection of craft, design and contemporary art. He was previously Director of the Museum of Arts and Design, Head of Research at the V&A and Curator at the Chipstone Foundation in Milwaukee. Adamson's publications include *Thinking Through Craft* (2007); *The Craft Reader* (2010); *Postmodernism: Style and Subversion* (2011, co-edited with Jane Pavitt); *The Invention of Craft* (2013); and *Art in the Making* (2016, co-authored with Julia Bryan-Wilson); and *Fewer Better Things: The Hidden Wisdom of Objects* (2018). His new book, *Craft: An American History*, will be published by Bloomsbury in January 2021.

LOUIS DE BERNIÈRES

immortalized as the creator of the global bestseller, *Captain Corelli's Mandolin,* was born in London and selected as one of the 'Best Young British Novelists' on the 1993 Granta list. Known for his immersive, picaresque fiction, de Bernières first novels formed a loosely connected sequence set in Latin America: *The War of Don Emmanuel's Nether Parts*; *Señor Vivo and the Coca Lord* and *The Troublesome Offspring of Cardinal Guzman.* The success of Corelli ensured he need never work again, yet he followed it up a decade later with *Birds Without Wings*, a Turkish epic inspired by *War and Peace.* De Bernières said of it, 'I'm one of those writers who's always going to be trying to write War and Peace: failing, obviously, but trying.' More recently, his works include *A Partisan's Daughter*; *The Dust That Falls from Dreams* and 2018's much-anticipated *So Much Life Left Over.*

STEFANIE BACH

is a curator for Global Art History specializing on Africa at the Staatliche Ethnographische Sammlungen Sachsen (State Ethnographic Collections of Saxony), which belong to the Staatliche Kunstsammlungen Dresden (Dresden State Art Collections), Germany. She was a curatorial assistant at the Museum für Völkerkunde Dresden and the GRASSI Museum für Völkerkunde zu Leipzig from 2017 to 2019. At the Staatliche Ethnographische Sammlungen Sachsen she was involved in exhibition projects such as *Working Space Prolog; Prolog #1-10 - stories about people, things and places; Made in Africa; Woman to Go, Megalopolis I - Voices from Kinshasa* and the reopening of the restoration laboratory of the Damascus Room for the public in 2019. She studied Art History, Non-European Cultures and Global Art History with a focus on Africa in Leipzig (Universität Leipzig) and Berlin (Freie Universität Berlin). In addition to the conceptualization of exhibition formats, her research interests include decolonization processes within the museum landscape as well as the accessibility, barrier-free access and mediation of museum content.

NADANIA IDRISS

is an art historian with a love for social work. She founded the non-profit organization Berlin Glas e.V. in 2011, and established Berlin Glassworks GmbH in 2015. Born in Berkeley, California, she has a specialization in medieval art and architecture of the Middle East. She moved to Paris in 1997 and worked at UNESCO until she moved to Berlin in 2005. Nadania discovered and fell in love glass at Pilchuck Glass School near Seattle in the early 1990's. Berlin Glas e.V. runs outreach programs for children and adults focusing on underserved communities, teaches a university class in conjunction with the two largest art academies in Berlin and offers residencies for visiting artists. Berlin Glassworks is a for-profit company offering classes to the general public, specialized workshops for universities and public schools, and, since 2018, the lighting label ANALOG.

MARIAM ROSSER-OWEN

is the curator of the Middle East collections at the Victoria and Albert Museum, London. She specializes in the arts of the medieval Islamic Mediterranean, particularly Spain and North Africa, and is the author of *Islamic Arts from Spain* (London: V&A Publishing, 2010). Since 2015, she has been undertaking a research and acquisition project on contemporary crafts of the Middle East, funded by Art Fund's New Collecting Awards. She organized an international conference on this theme at the V&A in October 2018, and also guest-edited a special issue of the *Journal of Modern Craft* (31:1, March 2020). She curated the display of *Perched* in the V&A's Jameel Gallery from June 2018-April 2019 and is now putting together an exhibition on *Contemporary Ceramic Art from the Middle East*, which will open in the V&A's Ceramics Galleries in November 2020.

PROF. DR. STEFAN WEBER

is the Director of the Museum of Islamic Art at the Pergamon Museum in Berlin, Germany. Previously, he was Assistant Professor of Material Culture at Aga Khan University in London. Between 1996 and 2007 he was a Research Fellow at the German Archaeological Institute (DAI) in Damascus and at the Orient-Institut in Beirut (OIB). He is currently organizing the re-conceptualization of the Museum of Islamic Art. His focus lies on the accessibility of the museum for the general public, and he has initiated several community programs. His Multaka program, which trained refugees as guides for the museums, has won several awards. He has curated larger exhibitions and has conducted research as well as an award winning restoration and documentation projects on cities and the cultural heritage of the Middle East. His academic profile combines the fields of material culture as well as Islamic art and history in projects ranging from the Umayyad period to early modern cities in Syria and Lebanon. Prof. Dr. Weber is a member of the international board of the Congress of Turkish Art, corresponding member of the German Archaeological Institute, member of the International Council on Monuments and Sites (ICOMOS) and other relevant organizations. He published widely on Middle Eastern heritages and is Honorary Professor at the Freie University Berlin.

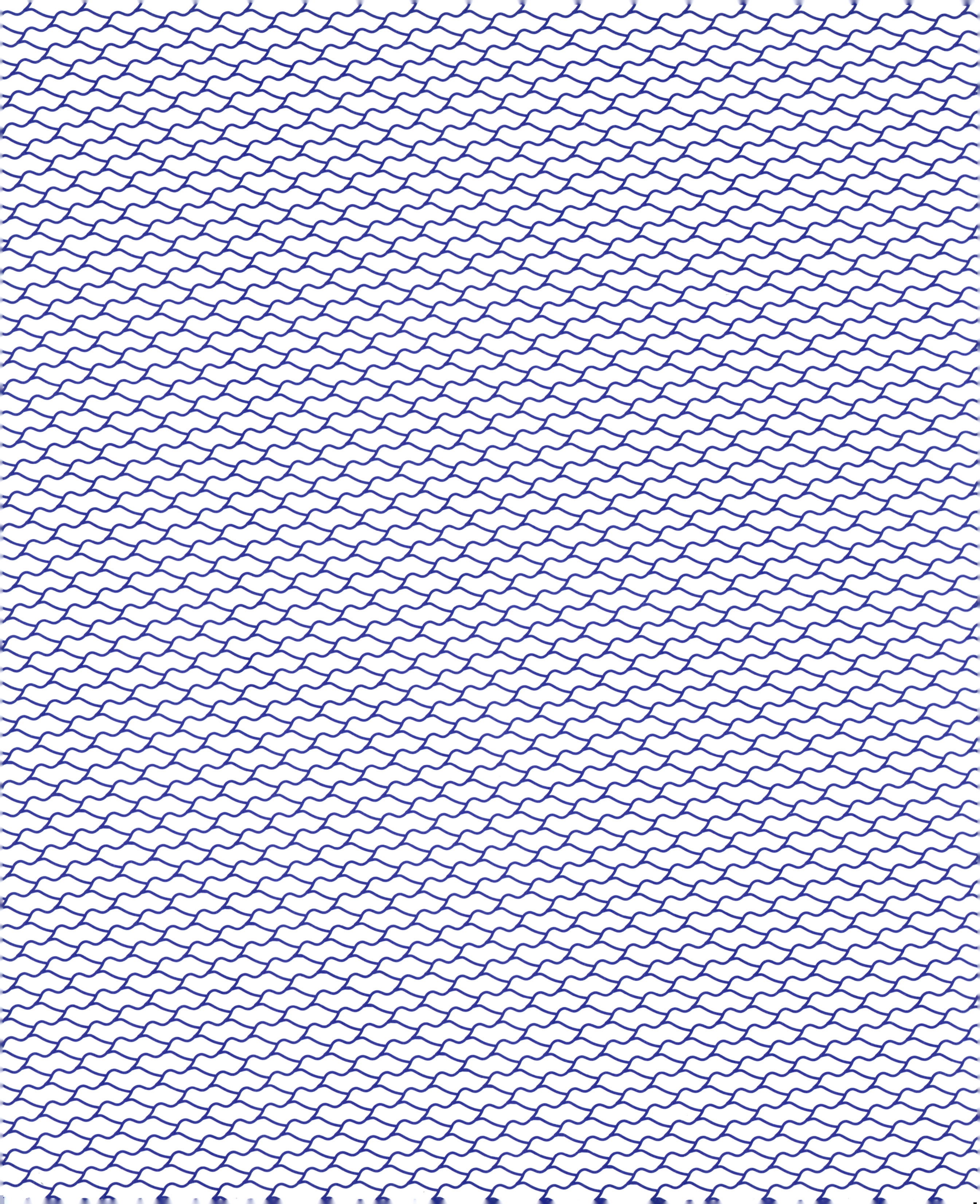